The Investor's Guide to
Vintage Character Collectibles

REX MILLER

Published by

700 E. State Street • Iola, WI 54990-0001
Telephone: 715/445-2214

Please call or write for our free catalog.
Our toll-free number to place an order or obtain a free catalog is 800-258-0929
or please use our regular business telephone 715-445-2214
for editorial comment and further information.

Library of Congress Catalog Number: 98-84628
ISBN: 0-87341-609-0
Printed in the United States of America

Table of Contents

Introduction

The Collectibles Market: Yesterday, Today and Tomorrow

A quarter-century ago, the word "collectibles" came into popular usage. When we talked to the average update antique store in Heartland, USA, we no longer found a lot of antiques. We saw glassware, furniture and (for the lack of a better term) stuff. Antiques and heirloom pieces were vanishing from the scene. Primitive trestle tables and early glassware gravitated toward the priceiest galleries and shops or was in private collections or museums. Many antique stores—in truth—were used furniture shops. So this is what happened: A lot of people realized they could sell antiques if they had some and if they weren't so doggone high priced, so they had artisans make some more. Thus, the reproduction was born.

By the early- to mid-1960s, the youth of the buyer with discretionary income (and the tone of the marketplace) began to further evolve, seemingly in direct proportion to all the repros and influx of pieces coming from the Mexican, British and European markets. The result was a new fascination with and mainstream acceptance of "collector's items" and "Americana" from the popular culture. These were collectibles that someone in the average income strata could hope to find and buy at a reasonable price.

Things had started changing much earlier with the post-war Baby Boom. And just as the traditional family structure change, so did traditional job and investment markets. Dad no longer held the same job for 30 years. As we fast forward from the 1960s through the 1980s (the counter-culture, Civil Rights movement, Viet Nam, Watergate, drugs, the Iran hostage crisis, inflation, Reganomics, the Japanization of the U.S. economy, the Federal deficit, the S&L scandal, the future of Social Security and worries about the cost of medical care), character collectibles and Americana was looked at with a fresh perspective. It became clear that the new collectibles and Americana field was one in which people were investing and making money doing so.

I always collected something, even as a kid. By 1954, while working in small-market radio, I amassed a huge collection of radio program transcriptions, which were my trade goods when my personal interests widened to embrace premiums, toys, films and serials, posters, advertiques, small format books and comic art—character collectibles from various dream merchants of childhood.

In the mid-1960s, I was corresponding with and somewhat tentatively buying from one or two dealers specializing in Golden Age comic books, strips and related memorabilia. Among them was the top dealers in the country—the late Phil Seuling. At some point, I managed to amass a grand sum of $500 cash, and I mustered sufficient nerve to buy a small collection from Phil's vast stock. He sold me a set of first-issue comic books which included about 50 of the top 100 titles and another 100 or so pristine mint books from D.C. and Timely. The two lots were $250 each. I quickly sold them for what seemed like a big profit and went on to become a full-time dealer in nostalgia collectibles.

That same pair of pots I purchased from Phil way back when, for a whopping $500, would sell today for $2 million-$3 million. Would you care to tell me one of your horror stories? Actually, I enjoy remembering that time and many other such purchases from Phil over the years. It was a great learning experience, and I share this with you to illustrate how character collectibles have appreciated in the intervening 30 years.

Collectibles in general have only one direction to head as the supply of authentic items continues to dwindle—straight up. Today's $300,000 super rarity will probably be worth $500,000 by the year 2003. As crazy that might sound, look at the track record of these goods. They've become the hard-money standard for many of us who trade in the collectibles vineyards. Premiums, toys, comics, posters and art are already buying homes and new vehicles, paying for lavish vacations and putting kids through college—all which ensures the future of savvy collectors. As I will point out to you carefully in this book, there's no worse reason to collect than to take a profit—but if you love something and you are going to collect anyway, you might as well learn to do it well and do it profitably.

The future for collector items look bright. Every day, more people look for top collectibles and it becomes increasingly difficult to find better quality memorabilia. Prices seldom even hit a momentary lull on the top-of-the-line memorabilia. I can only think of a few examples of such market drops or lulls in three decades of active trading: (small format books, base-ball cards and some of the characters so over-promoted (G.I. Joe, Barbie), that people go caught up in the fury to buy "at any cost" and without regard to the item's relative worth.

This book is no essentially about the appreciation of or the enjoyment one can find in collecting character memorabilia, it is about how to buy and sell such good so that a person might actually make money and have fun while he or she collects. If you collect initially because you love the items, you can invest in a way that will make you significant profits. I'm going to try to show you the way to do that meaningfully.

History and Buzz

Each chapter the book opens with several bites of information, including the "History" of the particular character, followed by some or all of the following:

The Buzz: What is the marketplace saying about the character. What makes a character "cook" and "sizzle."

Buy it now: Item(s) that are sleepers, HTF and really hot for the future that you should make special effort to purchase now.

Buy it later: Item(s) that are common, easy to find or unpopular that you should wait to buy.

Watch out: Advice on repros and other mistakes to avoid.

The Value Factors

I'm going to be wrong some of the time, and I will point out this fact again to reemphasize it in the strongest possible language. My crystal ball is as cloudy as the next guy's. I have a track record for making substantial profits, but the one time you trust my judgment, you could lose big, so buy only with extreme caution. Listen to your gut instincts. Use common sense and your own good taste.

With that said, let me explain the methodology used in this book. I will list one or more random items ("Rex Selections") from the hottest characters, by chapter; sometimes, where applicable, by genre or category; then my current appraisal of the item's worth, its projected value in the year 2004; followed by the three factors of "Collectiblity," "Scarcity" and "Investibility. These three numbers will be totaled as the factor representing its overall market worth. I'll grade from 1 (low) to 10 (high) in the three categories (Collectiblity, Scarcity and Investibility), If the total of the points in the three categories is 30, I consider it "money in the bank."

Here is what this will look like throughout the book:

Rex Selections

Item	1999	2004	CF	SF	IF	TF
1. Jimmie Allen Air Adventures cloth banner/valance	$1,000	$2,000	10	10	10	30

       Item: Describes the item
       1998: Value of the item in 1999
       2003: Projected value of the item in 2004
       CF: Collectibility Factor
       SF: Scarcity Factor
       IF: Investibility Factor
       TF: Total Factor (sum of CF, SF and IF)

Condition: With but a few exceptions, the prices quoted for items in this book are original or "pristine mint." Mint is supposed to apply only to metallic items, as in "bright, uncirculated" coinage. But most collectors accept the misnomer and we'll say "mint" for all 99% of the things in this book, including paper and plastic items. Collectors who pay top prices seek only the top condition; so should we.

Here are the factors, beyond condition, that figure into the supply-and-demand formula:

Collectiblity Factor

The collectibility of a given character collectible has nothing whatsoever to do with either the rarity or the future worth of the memorabilia. Some characters—the famous space heroes of the Golden Age, for example—are intensely collectible. Superman, Batman, the singing cowboys of the B-movies and TV, serial and comic book stars such as The Shadow and The Green Hornet, are major collectibles. Everyone knows that Howdy Doody, Hopalong and the Amazing Spider-Man are highly collectible. Why? That's the more difficult to define and isolate.

Some names kept their fame over the years while other stars faded into black. In 1941, and through the war years, the radio character Scattergood Baines, a cracker-barrel philosopher and sometimes-sleuth, was so popular that his stories were made into a series of moderately successful feature films by RKO Radio Pictures. He even made it to TV. But who has heard of Scattergood Baines today? Such characters are said to have "stiffed out." They're no longer collectible.

Scarcity Factor

The relative scarcity of an item is—by itself—of almost no relevance in determining the future value of that item. The scarcity of something is far less important than its condition, which almost always has a direct effect on the potential worth of collectible goods. That item's rarity only becomes a component in the price/value equation if the "Collectibility" and "Investibility" factors are present.

Here's a tale of two pins made in the 1930s: One is a "Hello Big Boy" pin issued by the makers of Amos 'n' Andy Candy; the other is a "Stoopnocracy is Peachy" pin offered by the radio show Stoopnagle & Budd. The latter pin is ultra rare but from a radio show that is long forgotten and not collectible. Scarcity notwithstanding, the Stoopnagle & Budd pin is considered a "stiff." The Amos 'n' Andy pin is common, but most of us would gladly pay $20 or more for it.

Investibility Factor

This category is ever changing, as the marketplace in character collectibles evolves over time. Unlike general "Collectibility" and "Scarcity," it *totally* resists numerical explanation. In fact, if you were to make a contrived formula based on the first two factors along, the end result would inevitably be skewed. The interpretation of overall market conditions is 1) subjective; and 2) always shifting. No two people, regardless of experience, will agree in such interpretive matters. If anyone knew the future, he or she would be a billionaire. Predicting value is at worst, guesswork; at best, a highly imperfect science. For the most part, assessing "Investibility" is a matter of feel, taste and track record. Therefore, one's personal background is sure to be a big influence.

I've tried to keep the emphasis on my own areas of expertise, where I know the strongest market elements are, and on what appear to be sure bets. I'm going to be wrong some of the time, so be forewarned. Take lunch boxes, for instance. It looks like there's no end in sight to their climbing values. From Beany and Cecil in vinyl to the earliest tin cowboy sets, top merchandise is already heading toward the thousands; from a mainstream standpoint, the lunch box market seems hotter than ever. That's today. As the better boxes get more and more difficult to find and Baby Boomers grow older, who can say? So one makes general statements like: "Buy as close to mint at you can. Try to buy with the thermos. Buy the best, even when prices seem prohibitive." Similarly, in some areas, I have no expertise whatsoever, so where books already exists (cookie jars, trading cards in boxes, dolls and so on), you'll find I've concentrated on other goods.

This late-1970s Superman lunch box is a real eye-pleaser.

Your taste, common sense and visceral reactions *can* be trusted over any price guide. I know next to nothing about the Investibility of New Age lunch boxes, but this Superman lunch box speaks volumes:

- *Superman is the hottest character in collecting.*
- *Lunch boxes is an ever growing field.*
- *This set is in original condition with a mint thermos*
- *It's 20 years old and getting older as you read this.*

If the price seems reasonable, affordable and you like the piece, you *know* it's got to be money in the bank. Plus, look at the fun you'll have displaying it.

The X-Factor

The same rules that apply to general collector's items, such as aesthetic value, supply, demand and price do *not* apply universally in pop culture artifacts. A component goes into the "Investibility of a specific collectible that sometimes defies logic and resist pigeon-holding. I'll call it "The X-Factor." For example:

A pair of badges in relatively small number, a rare variation of Jimmie Allen's Flying Cadet Wings and a Doc Savage Gold Medallion Honor Award. Each is from the 1930s. They are equally sought by collectors of their respective characters. Jimmie's badge (the rarer of the two) goes for about $200, while you can trade one version of Doc's medallion for a new Lincoln Continental. The X-Factor is in action.

Let's examine a few serial posters where the "X" marks the spot:

Hot	Not
Adventures of Captain Marvel (1941)	Adventures Smilin' Jack (1943)
The Batman (1943)	The New Adventures of Batman and Robin (1949)
Dick Tracy (1937)	Dick Tracy Returns (1938)
Flash Gordon (1936)	Flash Gordon Conquers the Universe (1940)
The Spider's Web (1938)	The Spider Returns (1941)

That's the X-Factor at work.

This "Blackhawk" poster starring Kirk Alyn is worth far less than a "Superman" poster starring Alyn. That's the X-Factor at work.

Superman posters starring Kirk Alyn will have collectors getting into serious four-figure bidding wars, bit you'll have trouble getting $400 for Alyn as "Blackhawk," who is highly collectible but lacks that X-tra something.

You might think that the same folks who would pay from $5,000-$8,000 for a Superman blue version of the 1940 Marx Rollover Plane in the box would be equally excited about a Superman Crime Fighters belt and buckle with original paper. Thing again! As you collect and gain X-perience, I predict you'll start your own personal X-files of such apparent trivia. X-es aside, all the items we've just discussed qualify as perfect "30s." Go figure.

In some ways, the mystery of why people collect what they collect (more to the point, why they pay such seemingly outrageous prices for things they want) is an enigma far more complex than any X-Factor. The "why" is not definable and varies as much as our individual personalities. Certainly, among the more obvious reasons is to recapture something that was pleasurable: a toy, gadget ring, comic book or radio program, TV premium or a film experience. It's wanting to "freeze" a moment in time with some tangible reminder that will act as a memory trigger. Just as often it's because we want to acquire something we never had but wanted desperately. My cousin Woodsen used to always tell me, "I'm still waiting for my Kix Atomic Bomb Ring from The Lone Ranger!"

In this book—a guide for investing in collectibles, as well as collecting for the fun and joy it—we will speak of market maxims, and new-comers might be led to believe that this stuff is so high high-priced today that their favorite collectibles are out of reach or so pricey that they can no longer be resold for a profit by anyone but a veteran dealer. Neither is an accurate assumption. I'll show you how to spot some of the astounding bargain prices that can still be found rather easily with regard to mid-range collector's items.

We'll examine market "heat" and talk about a given character's "buzz," as we learn to separate

Which has more X? The Superman Rollover Plane has a huge X-vantage over the Superman belt and buckle.

the "Bat Gold" from the "Bat Guano." You'll learn such stuff as which radio comedian's boxed board game sells for $1,000…secrets most collectors still haven't learned about The Avenger and Mighty Mouse…how you can get some ultra-valuable "hot Flashes"…and just who *was* that masked man. (Sorry, Kemo Sabe, it wasn't The Lone Ranger.) Also included are "Insider Q&A's" from leading collectors and media stars—questions we asked and they answered or vice versa. By the time the smoke clears, we hope you'll find this book to be a road map to the main streets and back alleys of pop culture; a map that will aid you in collecting wisely. But most of all, we hope that this guide will ensure you have a fun trip!

Auctions, Abbreviations and Horror Stories

Because we'll often be talking about "top-line merch" and market "max," let's dispel one myth early on: One-on-one sales are seldom in the same rarefied prices ranges as those auction sales generate. It's currently stylish to denote by an asterisk (*) auction prices when they appear in guides. We don't do that for one simple reason: More often than not, private sales on top-line goods rival or exceed those achieved by the big auction houses. Private sellers simply choose not to promote the sales they've achieved.

In some instances, an extremely high price has been produced by an auction bidding war between two or more aggressive collectors or dealers, and so we've noted that fact. If you enter into such a bid-

ding war, be it large or small, you'd better be very sure of what you're doing. And it had best be with an auctioneer you know and have found reliable.

I'm going to tell you some of the recommended reading sources for a would-be investor in character items, the foremost of these is *Toy Shop*. This bi-weekly magazine is the place where all the smaller auctioneers display their wares (excluding comics, art and screen-related collectibles). *Toy Shop* is an on-going training ground for a neophyte or very advanced buyer. When you're dealing with an auctioneer the first time, be sure you fully understand all of their terms, particularly with respect to: authenticity, condition and return policy. How carefully have they established provenance on an item? How strictly is it graded? What happens if you receive the item and isn't in the condition described?

There are a zillion pitfalls in collecting, and one never learns them all. For example, you see an ad for rare original pulp art. You pay a big price and it is by the artist who actually drew that character in the 1930s, but it was drawn in the last years of their life and it is unpublished piece since the pulp for which it would have been intended had long been discontinued. What happens if the seller claims—correctly—that your *interpretation* of his ad was wrong…that he never claimed it was artwork from the Golden Age? Are you stuck?

At times like this, you'll be smart to have done all your homework before you waded into the auction arena. Don't be afraid to phone an auctioneer in advance and ask all the questions you need to be prepared to bid. If you have collector friends, ask them which dealers and auction houses have the best record of dealings. We're all in this together, and there is no reason to operate in a vacuum.

Every field has a major show of some kind or a convention, such as the Sand Diego Comic Con or Pulpcon. Watch for these events. If you have a local club devoted to your favorite hobby, join it, even if you aren't a "joiner." The more information and intelligence you can gather, the better off you'll be.

Abbreviations

You'll encounter some abbreviations and jargon as you turn these pages. Here are some of the more common ones you'll run across:

BLB: This originally stood for Big Little Books or Better Little Books, but now refers to all Whitman, 5-Star Library, Goldsmith, Cup Lid Book, Dell Fast Action or any other small-format publication bigger than a gum booklet.

HTF: Hard to find, or VHTF (very hard to find).

Mint: As I mentioned, "mint" will be used to denote original condition or uncirculated, and has nothing to do with coins.

Repros: Reproductions.

SASE: Self-addressed stamped envelope

The Mysterious Island" is an example of a 24-sheet, which is 9 feet by 22 feet in size, and valued at $10,000. (photo courtesy of Butterfield & Butterfield)

Movie paper: This is based on a billboard being "24 sheet," so a very large poster is called a "6-sheet," typically 81 x 81 inches. The smaller posters are "1-sheets" (11 x 14 inches), and "half-sheets" (22 x 28 inches), and we could fill a page with bewildering sizes such as standees, shelf displays, day bills, door panels, valences, banners, broadsides, midget window cards and so on. In most cases, the size of a movie items will be included in any ad or catalog. If it isn't, ask.

A "Horror" Story

Large signage, such as character billboards, 6-sheets and 3-sheets, diecut stand-ups, standees and other outsized pieces are one of the most undervalued areas of character collectibles. Nobody has room to display in their homes, and these rarities often go begging for buyers. *A smart collector can make a small fortune with large pieces.*

Let's examine two recent sale items: 6-sheets sold by the auction house Butterfield & Butterfield in California. They each sold in the thousands, as horror 6-sheets are all but impossible to find, but the point is that there was almost not way the respective buyers could have overpaid. The 81 x 81-inch color posters were for "Frankenstein Meets The Wolfman" (a double-star 1940s classic) and "Creature from the Black Lagoon" (arguably the hottest current horror title of the Silver Age, 1950s).

I consider it a bungled opportunity on my part that I didn't bid on these two items. My reasoning was that I didn't have anywhere to store them, a reason that was somewhere south of "moronic." I guess the phrase "cold storage" is beyond my parameters. In any event, I passed. *Dumb.*

Consider this scenario: It is the year 2004. A major corporation (night club, theme park, restaurant chain) decides to decorate a large area in horror posters. Do you have a clue as to what kinds of prices the last big "Frankenstein" and "Dracula" pieces brought. Major buck, folks! Rock star money. What can I tell you? I blew it.

Books and Periodicals

Reading is a terrific tool for any hobbyist. Here are the many books and periodicals I recommend, per your area of interest:

Do you remember radio? Real radio? America once gathered in darkened living rooms and parlors, the only light coming from the amber glow of a gothic console model Philco, to listen to the crackling, chilling resonance of The Shadow, the piercing staccato of Terry & the Pirates, the thrill-packed excitement of The Adventures of Superman! Radio spawning many of the most collectible characters of today. A book that old-time radio collectors regard as important to the era was ***The Big Broadcast***. It was the first of many such books that contain radio broadcast references (*Tune in Tomorrow*, etc.), which may be available in a revised edition when you read this. If not, books such as these are often available through booksellers who carry used or out-of-print books. The original edition was printed in 1966 by Rank Buxton and Bill Owen, both of whom were around when the hobby of old show collecting caught hold. *The Big Broadcast: 1920-1950* is pub-

The author says he "blew it" when he didn't bid on the 6-sheets of "Frankenstein Meets The Wolfman" and "Creature from the Black Lagoon." (photos courtesy of Butterfield & Butterfield)

lished by Avon Books, 959 Eighth Ave., New York, NY 10019.

If you love periodical books, one of the radio- and pulp-era books to look for is Walter B. Gibson's *The Shadow Scrapbook*. It's out of print and HTF, but well worth the time, trouble and expense. The graphic art of *The Shadow Magazine* is like a ticket to a time machine.

Since its inception, Robert M. Overstreet's *The Comic Book Price Guide* has been the standard for collectors. It covers every area of comic book collecting, from the earliest comics to New Age merchandise. Various editions of this guide have focused on the amazing upward climb of values, with an eye toward dispensing accurate investor data. Even the first edition of the publication itself is now very collectible. Market reports, the care and handling of collector's comics, conventions, clubs, fanzines and how to begin a collection—all can be found in Overstreet's book. This book is a must-have for comic book character collectors. If your local bookseller does not carry the book, contact Overstreet Publications, 780 Hunt Cliff Dr. NW, Cleveland, TN 37311; or Gemstone Publishing Inc., 1966 Greenspring Dr., Timonium, MD 21093. To ensure you get a response, enclose an SASE.

Detectibles, collector's items related to the classic sleuths, are among the most fascinating of character items to pursue, and hunting the by-products of the famous manhunters can be a challenge. Several important and highly readable reference works exist, but for basic info on print and film 'tecs, two titles have been

indispensable: *Famous Movie Detectives* (by Michael R. Pitts, 1979, The Scarecrow Press, Inc., Metuchen, NJ). If this book is out of print, I suggest making an effort to find a copy. It's well researched on the film sleuths, excluding a few names where many works already existed on that character at the time it was published (notably, Sherlock Holmes).

The other book that I recommend is *Encyclopedia of Mystery and Detection* (1976, McGraw-Hill, Orlando, FL). This comprehensive work, edited by Chris Steinbrunner and Otto Penzler, runs the gamut of well-known and obscure characters, and it contains detailed biographies on many authors, as well. The degree of research is impressive in each of these books, especially in terms of film and print collectible titles.

Robert M. Overstreet, mentioned earlier, is also responsible for a couple of other great publications: *Hake's Price Guide to Character Toy Premiums*, a monumental work jam-packed with photos and values; and *The Overstreet Toy Ring Price Guide* from Overstreet and Gemstone Publishing are must-reads if you're interested in premiums, toys, character advertising and/or rings. These books are available in trade editions. For more info, write to Gemstone Publishing Inc., 1966 Greenspring Dr., Timonium, MD 21093.

Do you remember chapter plays? The world of movie serials has been covered in several books worth owning. If you want to recapture the eras of Spy Smasher and Flash Gordon, a well-researched book of illustrated synopses for chapters of the

1929-1956 period is: *To Be Continued...* (by Ken Weiss and Ed Goodgold, 1981, Star Tree Press, Stratford, CT). I believe this book is out of print, by try to find it through used or collector booksellers.

For photo-journalism, I'd buy anything with **Alan Barbour's** name on it, as I've enjoyed every I've ever read by him on the old B-movies and "cliffhangers."

Your special areas of interest in character collectibles may already be served by a newsletter, ad-zine or fanzine. An "ad-zine" is a kitchen-table or lap-top publication probably done on a regular basis by a collector or collector-dealer like yourself. It typically will be light on text or stories, but will be filled with ads placed by other collectors and/or dealers on your favorite subjects. Classified ads, often inexpensive, are a good source for beginning collectors who are looking for specific characters or items. Lap-top publications can be very sophisticated in scope, style and appearance or the ad-zine may be a photocopied list that was simply typed and stapled or even handwritten. Some of the major publications such as *The Comic Buyer's Guide* began life a quarter-century ago as a homemade ad-zine. Some example of seminal fanzines (the 1933 publication of Science-Fiction) command prices to rival those of first- and key-issue comic books.

There are many ways to seek out sources for newsletters and the like, but none better than your local public library, which may or may not have a user-friendly reference department. If it has one, get hold of a newsletter directory. At last count, there were 4,000 to 5,000 newsletters offered in business and hobby-related subject matter. Newsletters, even primitive home-grown varieties, often have ads filled with scarce memorabilia and will be a vital source for data about upcoming events, new publications and advice to aid all experience-level collectors. If there isn't an newsletter that satisfies your area (s) or collecting, perhaps there's a need for one. With the help from other collectors-dealers, you could start up your own newsletter.

There is one area that is in dire need of such a newsletter—premiums. As far as I know, there is no regularly published newsletter on premiums. The technology to publish a good quality newsletter on premiums, giveaways and sendaways exists today, and I know I would enjoy subscribing to a well-documented, professionally photographed premium 'zine of some kind. I asked Fred Gooses, the executive director of The Newsletter Association in Washington, DC, how much it takes to put together a small hobby newsletter. He said $4,000 at a minimum. I think it could be done cheaper than that. The Newsletter Association sells its own 272-page book

called *Success in Newsletter Publishing* (703-527-2333), but a careful scan of other successful kitchen-table publications will prove instructive.

You might also contact trade association, such as the Direct Marketing Association in New York, or your own regional organizations, to get as much general information as possible on this subject. You could really build a major collection through self-published work, as a newsletter, flyer, catalog or other direct-mail pieces are wonderful if you have a trade list. Any reliable book broker can publish, produce and drop-ship or act as fulfillment shipper for homemade publications. One is the Newsletter Book Service at 800-382-0602.

Publishing a newsletter or 'zine is among the most consistently overlooked areas in character collecting, with a rich, untapped potential for the savvy collector. If you can figure a new slant on a business/hobby newsletter that takes aim at a virgin bullseye within the collectibles circle, and you test the market waters before you jump, you might just cash out big-time, as well as having one heckuva lot of fun in the process.

Another overlooked area is toll-free numbers. Twice a year, AT&T updates and publishes a massive Toll-Free Directory, also called Business Buyer's Guide. This sells for about $31 (800-426-8686). It lists about a godzillion different places where you can phone long distance for free, including many collectibles-related businesses. I have used this tool with great effectiveness. Once, when writing an article on how to get free things through the mail, I dialed several numbers and spent an hour or so on the phone seeing what people would send out gratis for publicity. I recall that one of the items was a cereal box flat that I later sold for $50. Believe it or not, I actually got a Thompson Sub-Machine Gun through these toll-free number! Admittedly, that was a unique deal, but you'll find the book is well worth the $31.

There are literally countless publications and price guides that have a hobby theme. There are even entire sections of antiques and collectibles papers devoted to nothing but books on every conceivable area of specified interest from beer cans to barbed wire. But over the years, I've found only a handful of periodicals to be of major significance for character collectibles. Foremost is *The Toy Shop*. If your areas of interest include virtually any character-related items, subscribe to this magazine. Here's where all the kitchen-table auctions are advertised; excluding comics and video items, the best goodies can be found on an entry-level basis. Here's where you'll see affordable (sometimes bargains) character collectibles. Another strong Krause Publications ti-

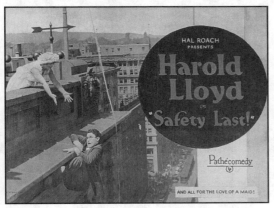

(Top left): A poster from "The General" sold for $17,000 and only a couple are known to exist. Shown here is a color lobby card; (top right): Everyone want to get their hands on paper items from "King Kong." (photo courtesy of Christie's); (bottom left): An 11 x 14-inch lobby card from "Safety Last" starring Harold Lloyd is a hot item. (photo courtesy of Butterfield & Butterfield); (bottom right): An original "King Kong" lobby car represents a character collectible with a solid gold future. (photo courtesy of Christie's)

tle is *The Comic Buyer's Guide*. It's a major source for buying and selling old comic books. **Krause Publications, 700 E. State St., Iola, WI 54490-0001, 800-258-0929.**

The Antique Trader Weekly has been a good buying and selling source for me for the last 30 years. The Trader also publishes an excellent film 'zine called *Big Reel* (strong in Western character collectibles). Also check out *Toy Trader*. **Antique Trader Publications, P.O. Box 1050, Dubuque, IA, 52004-1050, 800-334-7165.**

The Internet

This is an area I'm not that familiar with, but I do know it can be a place to find great information—there are many pages dedicated to particular character. Great fan pages with information and lists and other interesting tidbits. The Internet is also becoming an increasingly used area to buy and sell character collectibles. One of the top auction sites is at *eBay.com;* another is *collectit.ne.*. My same word of warning applies to the Internet as it does in any other medium of buying and selling. Be cautious and be sure of who you're dealing with.

The Foreign Market

The Investibility Factor becomes a complex matter where certain areas of character collectibles are concerned. High-ticket movie paper is a good example. Posters from the great comedians are fabulously collectible. Buster Keaton, Charlie Chaplin, Harold Lloyd and similar names from the silent era are gold in the marketplace, whether it's tin toys, tobacco items or figurines. Original paper from titles such as

"The General," "Spite Marriage," "City Lights," "Safety Last," etc., sells without a market maximum, and there is only so much material to go around. The same is true for collectibles from The Marx Brothers, Laurel & Hardy and other sound-era greats. A strong foreign market, therefore, is now being made in premium vintage poster art. This applies to any top paper, whether the genre is *film noir*, melodrama, science fiction or whatever. What it boils down to is this: Would you rather have an Australian daybill from the 1936 Flash Gordon serial or none at all?

All film buffs want original material from "Metropolis," "King Kong," "Gone with the Wind," "Duck Soup," "Modern Times," Casablanca," "The Maltese Falcon," "Steamboat Willie" and so on. Because so many collectors want the same thing, and because there is so little to go around, we have to make collecting compromises to own such material. The foreign market in rare paper is a hard reality, and top titles bring prices in the high thousands, but the tough question is: How much is too much? That's an individual decisions, but it's hard to make a case against foreign paper, It would *appear* that the investibility of this material will only solidify and grow.

In hard collectibles, there is a parallel market for English and European goods. Mickey Mouse and other Disney characters, superheroes, puppets, Western characters, Felix the Cat, Fleischer cartoon characters and dozens of famous images grace collector's items that seem to be selling as well as their U.S.-made counterparts. A few auction houses are now specializing in foreign material, and it is now often sold without country-of-origin identification. My personal feeling is that much of this material is overvalued and, with the exception of the very top-line collectibles, lacks investibility strength.

Confusing Collectibles

There are several areas where it might be easy to become confused in character collecting. For example, the name "The Octopus" is frequently used in print, film and over the air. Items that portray an octopus in a top hat are quite collectible, being from "Mysteries of Paris," which was Bourjois' early version of the vintage radio show "Evening in Paris."

Names can be confusing to neophyte collectors. "Silver" the horse might belong to The Lone Ranger or Buck Jones. The 1934 print sign entitled "Superman" turns out to be Doc Savage of the pulps. There were several "Junior G-Men"—it's a generic name, a name for one of the many variations of Dead End Kids, as well as Melvin Purvis's premium club.

"Junior G-Men" starring the Dead End Kids.

The octopus from "Mysteries of Paris."

Many character collectibles were not marked or tied-in to their print forms. Premiums which were offered on more than one radio show or in markets where licensing conflicts existed, were not identified. Jack Armstrong, The Lone Ranger, Hop Harrigan, The Green Hornet, Terry & the Pirates…there's a list that keeps going of these examples. Most collectors agree about the Kix Atomic Bomb Ring, but the most advanced dealers and collectors still dispute the character tie-ins on various rings.

Cardboard and paper toys were issued in as many forms as the market would justify. The big manufacturers such as Einsen-Freeman were famous for this. Sam Gold, legendary premium man, devised more than a dozen variations of the basic marble bomb toy. Some were tied-in to Jack Armstrong, Radio's Little Orphan Annie, Hop Harrigan, Captain Sparks and other characters from radio or comics.

Among the most difficult to find is the pair of cardboard cockpits Einsen-Freeman sold through

Bombsight version of the 1942 Einsen-Freeman cardboard cockpit toy.

Gunsight version of the 1942 Einsen-Freeman cardboard cockpit toy.

the comic books of World War II: One version features a bombsight set into a battle scene, while the other has a gunsight that targets Axis aircraft.

The Secrets of Collecting

1. *Only collect what you love.* Whatever the level of pursuit, remember that the worst possible reason to collect is to make money on your invested dollars.
2. *Do your homework.* Learn from folks who have "been there, done that." Collect smart. Don't collect in a vacuum. Ask questions. Much of the fun of the hunt is the learning process.
3. *Go with your gut instincts.* Nostalgia isn't what it used to be. Reworked items, repaints, repros and outright fakes—in every price range—are common. Trust your first reaction, especially on higher priced items. Feel froggy? Jump!
4. *Use caution when buying at auction.* Don't succumb to "bidding war fever" and overbid. Remember that "terms of sale" often tend to be as inflexible as a buyer's premium. Before you bid, be certain the auctioneer will *guarantee* provenance, and that all shipping details are clear in the case of absentee bidding.

Actually, the secrets to collecting anything can be summed up in one sentence: Use your good taste and common sense and you'll have happy hunting.

The Air Adventures of Jimmie Allen

1

History: Was his name Jimmie Allen or Jimmy Allen? Apparently neither his radio sponsors nor his publishers were sure, as memorabilia can be found with either name, but there was a *real* Jimmie, and the show was a super-hot sensation back in Kansas City in 1933. Skelly, Richfield and countless sponsors flooded the broadcast air with offers of wings, rings and Flying Cadet things of every kind.

The Buzz: The incorrect consensus is that he's a stiff, so super-scarce goods are relatively cheap. But diehard radio premium fans would love to have all the road maps, albums, I.D. bracelets and aviator gear if they could pick it up for pocket change. Every dealer in America has a Jimmie Allen badge for $15,

taking up space in a drawer. Cash in on the market misconception that Jimmie Allen is a dead issue. It's a great time to pick up the BLBs, mintish membership cards, knives, and secret signal code whistles with the little red and white string attached. Jimmie Allen super-collector Jack Deveny has this stuff already, so you might not have much competition.

Watch out: I don't know if the blotters have reproduced yet, but always beware that blotters, matchbooks and photos can be easily duplicated.

Buy it now: Here are four items to pick up in any acceptable condition (don't hold out for mint). We won't say that very often, but you'll be lucky to find the following in *any* presentable shape:

Rex Selections: The Air Adventures of Jimmie Allen

Item	1999	2004	CF	SF	IF	TF
1. Jimmie Allen Air Adventures cloth banner/valance	$1,000	$2,000	10	10	10	30
2. Jimmie Allen Official Outing Knife/Sheath	$400	$1,000	10	10	10	30
3. Air Adventures of Jimmie Allen Map of Countries Visited, 1934	$375	$650	9	9	10	28
* 4. Jimmie Allen Presentation Desk Set.	$750	$2,000	10	10	10	30
** 5. Tune In! blotter, Richfield Hi-Octane Gas	$75	$100	7	9	7	23
** 6. Rare version of Flying Club cards (dozens available)	$70	$100	7	9	7	23
** 7. Road Map of Missouri	$50	$75	7	9	6	22
** 8. Road Map of New York	$50	$75	7	9	6	22
** 9. *Jimmie Allen in the Air Mail Robbery* (BLB).	$30	$50	6	8	6	20
** 10. *Jimmy Allen* [sic] *in the Sky Parade*	$120	$140	6	8	6	20

* In spite of this piece having a Total Factor of 30 and a projected value of two grand by 2004, it's a piece to be cautious about. However rare, aesthetically pretty and collectible, this is for the completist collector and not necessarily the mainstream collecting buff. Translation: Unless you're a serious Jimmie Allen completist, would you really want to sink $750 into something that could be tough to sell, *if* you had to liquidate your collection?

** Items 5 through 10, buy only in perfect, original condition.

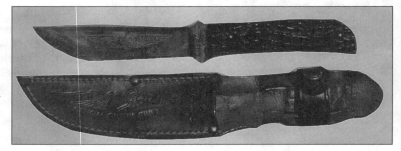

In this condition, the Jimmie Allen Official Outing Knife/ Sheath is valued at about $300. Even in this condition, it is a $750 item in 2003.

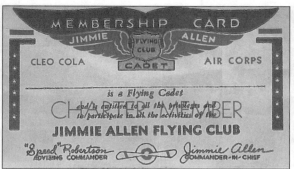 

Jimmie Allen Membership Card.

Road Map of Missouri.

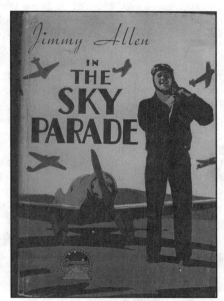

Jimmy Allen in the Sky Parade.

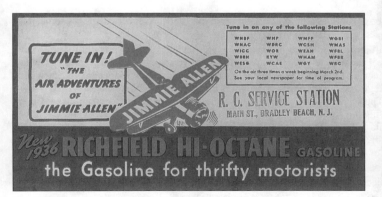

Jimmie Allen Tune In! blotter, Richfield Hi-Octane Gas.

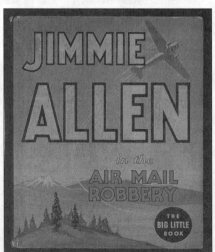

Jimmie Allen in the Air Mail Robbery.

2 *The Amazing Spider-Man*

History: Spidey's initial appearance was in "Amazing Fantasy No. 15," in 1962. Don't even ask what the premiere book is selling for in mint condition. He was forerunner of Marvel Comics' universe of humanistic superstars, spearheading a new trend in 1960s comic books. Created by Steve Ditko and the remarkable Stan Lee, Spider-Man's web of influence was of major importance to the industry's Silver Age.

The Buzz: His first- and key-issue comics are overpriced or at least priced up to what the market will bear and then some. The in the better artifacts, there are mega-bargains lurking.

Buy it now: Get the best Amazing Spider-Man collectibles you can find. Buy only pristine mint condition. Don't pay more than $500 for anything. Avoid bidding wars. The Amazing Spider-Man's Code Breaker is an example of a current steal in the marketplace—an item you can still find for pocket change that has a future four-figure potential…What? You don't call $300 pocket change?

Spider-Man Buddy-L Vehicles Set—a major league bargain at $300!

Buy it later: Coloring books, Spider-Hulk toilet paper, metal license plates for bicycles or your MG, jigsaw puzzles, wristwatches, sweatshirts, web-shooter…you get the idea.

Rex Selections: The Amazing Spider-Man

Item	1999	2004	CF	SF	IF	TF
1. Spider-Man Code Breaker	$300	$1,000	10	9	10	29
* 2. The Amazing Spider-Man Game	$400	$850	10	9	9	28
** 3. Spider-Man Buddy-L Vehicle Set	$300	$700	10	9	9	28
*** 4. Marvel eight-pin Superhero set, 1967	??	??	10	7	10	27
**** 5. Spider-Man premium ring	$75	$300	10	7	9	26

* This version of the Milton-Bradley game is important to collect in original *sealed* condition. Pay as much as $500 if you have to in mint.

** Get it unused and in the original window box. This was still selling in stores in the 1980s. As recent items go, some of the Spidey stuff is HTF. This is a great display piece.

*** This is one of the most complex sets of hero-related items to explain or rate. The Old X-Factor is definitely at work here. I can't estimate its value, in all honesty. I can only tell you it's a potential 30, if you can find it cheap enough. Spidey, Captain American, Silver Surfer, Sub-Mariner, Dr. Doom, Thor, The Fantastic Four and Hulk pinbacks pin down solid 10s in the Collectibility and Investibility categories, but the Scarcity Factor is difficult to rate. No one agrees on this set—only that its solid gold money in the bank. The scarcity level is from 6 to 10, depending on whose word you take. I'd say it's a mid-range piece in terms of rarity, giving it a soft and iffy Total Factor of 27. So what about current and future values. Your guess is as good as mine. I've paid $200 for the set and $2,000 for the set. I've sold it for hundreds of dollars and once for $3,000. Neither the buyer nor myself are sure to this day of anything except the fact that he and another guy has terminal bidding war fever for a couple of hours and the auctioneer made out like a bandit. Are you confused. Do you want your money back? (Sigh)

**** The Vitamins ring seems like a safe piece if you can pick it up cheap.

Watch out: Amazing Spider-man stuff is great to collect, but I'd be very careful buying pricier goods. This character's hardware exemplifies a category in which the high Investibility Factor is totally disproportionate to the low Scarcity Factor. But potential bargain areas make it worthwhile for you to study this part of the market closely and do your homework. Here are some way cool action figure prototypes from Sotheby's 1997 auction of comic books and comic art. These prototypical figures, sculpted by Cynthia Woodie in 1994, were offered by Sotheby's in the $1,400-$4,000 range. These are "money in the bank" collectibles if you've familiarized yourself with your hobby focus sufficiently.

1. Spider-Man Web Glider figure, red, blue and gray on a black base, 10-1/2 inches with hinged joints.
2. Spider-Man Black Costume figure, black and white, hinged, 10 inches (Alien symbiote, pre-Venom).
3. Multi-jointed Spider-Man, red and blue on a black base, 10-1/2 inches.
4. Battle-Ravaged Spider-Man figure, red, blue and black with shied on a black base, 10-1/2 inches.

Spider-Man Code Breaker.

Marvel eight-pin Superhero Set.

Box cover to The Amazing Spider-Man Game.

Inside of The Amazing Spider-Man Game.

3 *Batman*

History: In the beginning, Batman was "The Bat-man," the brainchild of artist Bob Kane and writer Bill Finger. Few heroes have had his "POW!" or staying power in the marketplace. The Caped Crusader of Gotham City was born in May 1939 issue of "Detective Comics," with a pedigree steeped in woodpulp, nitrate film and vintage air.

"The Bat" was a pulp character, a radio villain and the phantom heavy who killed from the shadows in silent films and, notably, in the 1931 old dark house talkie "The Bat Whispers." The Shadow himself was a major influence, and some say that Da Vinci's batwing sketches and the chapter play "Batmen of Darkest Africa" might have fed Kane's dark and batty imagery.

Batman's resurfacing in the 1960s in the retro showing of the old serials of the 1940s—and subsequent TV show that resulted—provided the touchstone for the nostalgia wave that washed over America around 1964. In the backwaters of 1966, the market saw a slew of bat merchandise, from red Batmobiles to Bat Guano, but the top stuff reflects the essence of the character.

The Buzz: Collectors have an insatiable appetite for the bat in tights. These classic collectibles get an A+, full-tilt-boogie rating from me on their scarcity, timeless design and universal appeal. The Dynamic Duo are every bit as hot today as they were when mainstream America rediscovered them in the mid-1960s.

Buy it now: Forget about "Detective Comics #27." A substandard, unrestored example fell under Sotheby's hammer for $60,000 recently. One in mintish shape would require a whole truckload of Ben Franklins from the mint itself. Restorable copies of "Batman Comics #1" still surface occasionally, albeit at what will seem like inflated price tags. This is such a strong book that it could sell without the front cover (see the highly flammable back-cover portrait)! That comic aside, go for the best obtainable condition.

Key books worth saving for are "Batman Comics #3," Fall 1940, contained the first costumed villainess in comics—The Catwoman (her origin and The Joker's took place in the spring of 1940 when "Batman #1" was on the newsstands). I also like "Batman Comics #8" with its classic infinity artwork; and "Batman Comics #27," the great 1945 Christmas cover issue marked "Back the 6th War Loan." Each of these come close to perfect 30s on the batscale.

Original art, signage, 1943-1949 serial posters, March of Dimes Postcard Portraits, a fabled Halloween costume from the Silver Age, playset in original boxes…you cannot lose, in my opinion.

Buy it later: Phonograph records, drinking cups, cardboard juice containers, iron-ons, paperbacks, pinbacks, rings, puppets, wastepaper baskets, magic slates, postcard from post-1966, mittens, puzzles, pajamas, stickers, decals, magazines with Batman covers, caps and hats, coins, ice cream containers, tableware, sneakers, cake decorations… junk, junk, junk, junk, junk, junk, junk, junk, junk, junk, junk, junk, junk, junk…

"Mask of the Phantasm Series" action figures from Kenner.

Watch out: The Ideal Playset has been reproduced, supposedly in limited numbers, but there are no controls on unlicensed repros. This whole area of collecting has become enormously perilous; it's a potential minefield for the uninitiated. First, do your homework. Second, get a signed, two-staged provenance with a no time-limit guarantee as to the authenticity of anything pricey you buy in the hero line. Hi-tech and high values create an arena that red flags the "entrepreneur" and hobby predator. Don't be a victim waiting to be ripped off. Third, do *more* homework. These pieces exist in more than one version and values vary with individual items. You may not now vinyl from vac-u-form, but if you're going to collect these things seriously, it would be a good idea to start asking questions…a lot of questions! Lastly, trust your instincts, above all else.

Early re-release 1-sheet from the 1943 chapters.

Bat Trivia: *What did the original Catwoman do for a living?* She was an airline stewardess!

Rex Selections: Batman

10 Bat Comics to look for

1. "Detective Comics #31" (1939). This is one of the moodiest, most mysterious and evocative of the early books. The cover is still the standard for Batman images of the Golden Age. One of pop culture's best collectibles.
2. "Batman Comics #1" (1940). Initial appearance of The Joker and The Catwoman.
3. "Batman Comics #3" (1940). See cover art.
4. "Batman Comics #4" (1940). Batman and Robin descending ladder over darkened Gotham City. Red sky background.
5. "Batman Comics #8." See cover art.
6. "Detective Comics #58." Initial appearance of The Penguin.
7. "Batman Comics #11." Batman and Robin playing-card cover.
8. "Detective Comics #140." Initial appearance of The Riddler.
9. "Detective Comics #33." Another classic Bat cover.
10. "Detective Comics #38." The first appearance of Robin, the Boy Wonder! Killer Kane at his most muscular.

Given the fact that these titles should be purchased in best obtainable condition, a current/projected valuation is meaningless. These are comics that thousands of collectors seek. Such titles in prime grade (the equivalent those from the Eugene Church Collection—Mile High Mint—it will be a seller's market when and if you find them. All of these comics are perfect 30s in near mint grade. It would be miraculous to find a near-flawless classic in what might currently be deemed a halfway reasonable price by 2004. If you have deep pockets and you are a serious comic book collector, consider the above books. Finally, any 1940s comic with Batman on the cover, in pristine condition, is money in the bank for both buyer and seller. Batman is the Chanel No. 5 of superheroes,

Each of the following collectibles is currently valued in the four-figure range and will probably double in the next five years:

11. 1942 War Bonds poster with Batman and Robin
12. 1943 The Batman 1-sheet serial poster
13. 1943 comic strip premium mask
14. 1943 March of Dimes Postcard Portrait for Infantile Paralysis Drive
15. 1944 Batman and Robin tattoo transfer sheets
16. 1950s (?) early Halloween costume (pre-Ben Cooper era version with gold lame utility belt)
17. 1949 New Adventures of Batman and Robin 3-sheet serial poster
18. Batman Playset by Ideal in original window box (see "Watch Out" section)
19. 1966 Batman Playset by plain box by Sears (larger version)
20. 1969 Burry's Cookies Batmobile dimensional sign

All of the above items are across-the-board perfect Total Factor 30s, with the exception No. 20, the sign, which is a 29.

Pieces like Fred Ray/Jerry Robinson Batman cover art, Adam West/Burt Ward costumes from TV, Batmobiles from TV and film features, Bat-props from serials, TV and movies, are items you can bank on, as they will likely only grow more valuable.

Item	1999	2004	CF	SF	IF	TF
* 21. 1966 Batman standee	$375	$575	10	8.5	7	25.5
* 22. 1966 Batman premium poster (with Robin)	$400	$750	10	9	10	29

* Nos. 21 and 22 show the X-Factor hard at work with Batman collector's items. Both are about the same price and each has the classic Batman pose. No. 22 is a solid 30 if you have the Robin poster. The X-Factor guarantees the future of the poster pair.

The next three items are collectibles worth investing in, but some aspect about them has driven me bats:

Item	1999	2004	CF	SF	IF	TF
* 23. 1966 Batman Utility Belt and Buckle on card	$200	$450	10	10	10	30
** 24. Batman Ideal Utility Belt with accessories	$1,000	$2,000	10	10	10	30
*** 25. Batman Remco Batmobile Dashboard	??	??	10	10	10	30

* No. 23 is on a nicely illustrated header card. It is remotely possible that there is an earlier version of this piece, as I've a couple over the years with lead-colored silver and brass finish rather than the red painted brass of the 1966 version; perhaps these were just worn 1966 versions. Joe Desris, *the* bat guy, doesn't think there were old variations on this toy, and I suspect he's correct. He know more about the masked man-hunter than Alfred the valet. What ever the case, if you can find the piece on the card for less than $200, you can double your money in a Gotham heartbeat.

** I think No. 24 is already overpriced at $1,000 or so, but it's got a strong future. I just don't like it.

*** I think No. 25 is a solid 30, but I have no idea of its true value. Oddly, I've never seen the piece. I've also never found a mint example of the Batman and Robin bookends. And how come they never made a Penguin umbrella gun. And why were there no Batman premiums in the 1940s. And how much wood could a wood chuck, chuck?

26. The last item on my list is actually an entire category. It's currently such a hot genre that it deserves a detailed mention, but it comes with a buyer's warning, so we could call it "Watch Out—Part 2: Batman Action Figures."

This is a category that dates back to the mid-1960s when Ideal came up with the character Captain Action; and the market was filled with everything from dolls with accessories to flicker rings that would change from Captain Action to The Phantom or Batman. Display-boxed figures could change the Captain into characters like Buck Rogers and Flash Gordon, The Lone Ranger and Tonto, and Superman and Batman. Mint-in-box Captain Actions with uniform and equipment complete and intact go for sky-high prices—$500 and into the thousands. To me, this is ridiculous. Why? I've got a couple of reasons—my eyes. These things look like junk. I don't care how scarce the stuff is.

Mego's Superhero action figures from the 1970s also strike me as rinky-dink nothings that are absurdly overvalued. I won't even start on the Toy Biz line. Megos to me are crude, silly looking, poorly designed and selling for *way* too much already. Line up all the junk action bat figures and shoot them with a batarang. Yikes! Junkaroony! Fo-git about it!

Kenner began cranking out Bat-folks in the 1980s, perhaps about the time the old syndicated cartoons of various DC superstars stopped running endlessly. Again, in the early-1990s, Kenner got into the act when "Batman: The Animated Series" went

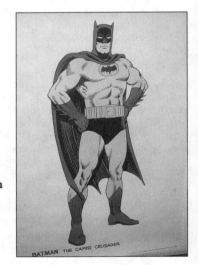

1966 Batman Premium Poster.

into release. It was an amazing animation adventure, deco-ish in feel and an obvious homage to Fleischer Studios impeccable 1940s Superman cartoon series, which, along with Terry's "Mighty Mouse," remained the 50-year-old standard for hero animation in color (Disney notwithstanding).

Some of the figures from that series are okay, but nothing to get all sweaty about. They were based on drawings, so the result was closer to the artwork than earlier action figures, but unless you had these things as a kid, I wouldn't recommend sinking any money into amassing a big collection.

A far more impressive grouping could be made of Batmobiles and other vehicles. It would be super-cool to see a row of 30 or 40 of these bad bat-boys on shelves. I'd concentrate on the cars, copters, planes, boars and such from 1966-1977. It's just my opinion. Like Dennis Miller says, "I could be wrong."

Better still, let's get back to a list of must-finds:

Item	1999	2004	CF	SF	IF	TF
27. Remco Magic Gotham City Playset, boxed.	??	??	10	10	10	30
28. Multiple Batman Justice League of America's Playset, boxed	$1,000	$2,000	10	10	10	30
29. Ideal Batman Playset, boxed	??	??	10	10	10	30
* 30. 1943 Standee from the Chapter Play	??	??	??	??	??	??

* This is basically a 3-sheet on hinged fiberboard and articulated.

Batman: Changes Through Time

The Batman of 1943.

The Batman from the second serial of 1949.

Burt Ward as Robin and Adam West as Batman at the wheels of the TV-era Batmobile, 1966.

Michael Keaton was a most unusual choice for the 1989 Batman film, but it worked!

History: Joe, the kid with the eye patch and base-ball cap, is all but unheard of by today's collectors. He was an advertising character saved from pop culture obscurity by the superbly conceived premiums that the gum company made available to kids who would save the little waxy cartoon panels that came with Bazooka Bubble Gum. The miniature comics sheets are extremely collectible, too, but the send-aways are just starting to take off big. It's cool stuff, fun to collect, still available "mint in mailer" and not real pricey, but it will be.

The Buzz: Every kid, young or old, who is into premiums, finds a torpedo-firing sub and exploding battleship irresistible. Talk about high concept!

Buy it now: Get all the rings while they're still plentiful.

Watch out: Don't overpay for items. Let's keep this in perspective—it's just kid's stuff, after all. The next thing you know, people will be selling old comic books for big money. What's the world coming to?

Rex Selections: Bazooka Joe

Item	1999	2004	CF	SF	IF	TF
1. Printing Ring with papers and print offer in original mailer . . .	$300	$500-$600	10	8.5	10	28.5
2. Initial Ring with papers and print offer in original mailer.	$250	$450-$500	10	8.5	10	28.5
3. Exploding Battleship with accessories/papers in original mailer	$175	$450	10	8	10	28

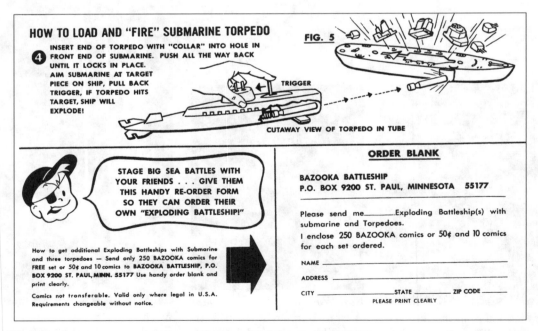

This $175 bubble gum sendaway will go up in value dramatically in the next five years.

Blondie

History: Blondie was Chic Young's baby, the evolution of his 1924 cartoon success, Dumb Dora. Six years later, the King Features Syndicate strip had a reputed 50 million readers of the daily panels gags. Blondie was also a natural for radio and films, and she was a big hit in the feature films of 1938, on the air in 1939, and later on TV. Band singer Dorothy McNulty, under the name of Penny Singleton, was a dead-solid perfect Blondie. Former child actor Arthur Silverlake, who, as Arthur Lake, had played such movie comic characters as Harold Teen in 1928, seemed to have been born to play the role of Dagwood Bumstead. Blondie (the quintessential blonde) and Dagwood (the symbol for a good-hearted, gutless oaf), are part of our culture. "Blondie" came back as a new wave-era band with Debbie Harry, and you still hear references to the towering "Dagwood" sandwiches.

The Buzz: Only film and toy collectors are in on the big secret about Blondie. She's hot. Smokin' hot! I'm on fire just thinking about finding a mint Blondie 3-sheet. To most everyone in mainstream collecting, she and Dagwood are stiffs. She the Jimmie Allen of the comics. Jack Armstrong…deadsville. Okay, but stand back and let the big dog eat.

Buy it now: If you can grab any top condition paper from the 1938 feature film, do so. It's pure gold. Radio premiums never surface, so even the "Blondie Goes to Leisureland" game from Westinghouse is worth getting because it will someday triple in value (it's currently cheap because a big hoard of them was dumped on the market). Jugates pinbacks with two images on the same pin, Esso folders, radio cast photos, boxes sets like the Comic Construction toy from 1934, can all be found occasionally at bargain prices. If you can find these items at a reasonable price, you will surely cash out nicely. *Keep in mind that at least 75% of dealers undervalue Blondie items at the current time.*

Buy it later: The boxed toys from the 1930s are already in the four-figure range, and I don't see much room in the post-1939 film paper. Smalls such as the Blondie and Dagwood rubberized plastic figures from Marx, the common stuff like lead pencils with metal bands, Pep pins, puzzles and the like will appreciate in value, but my advice is to pick up the hard-to-find items first.

Watch out: Toys are really pricey and—at the risk of being redundant, not to mention, repetitive— if you find yourself caught up in a bidding war for a mint boxed Blondie wind-up toy, chill out.

Blondie Trivia: *What was the name of the company Dagwood Bumstead worked for?* The J.C. Dithers Construction Company.

Blondie Dream Collectible: Here's a Blondie dream collectible…someday, if God decides you've been *real* good, he'll let you find a complete set of Blondie "Syrocco" (Syroco, pressed wood) statuettes, mint in the original Pillsbury Farina box from 1944. Since you'll only pay $15 for these worthless figures, you'll cheerfully sell the set to me for $60— quadrupling your investment, and we'll all be happy. I'll even send you a mint Dagwood Sandwich.

Rex Selections: Blondie

Item	1999	2004	CF	SF	IF	TF
1. "Blondie" 1-sheet, 1938, unused	$1,000	$4,250	10	10	10	30
2. Blondie and Dagwood Marx keywinds in original boxes, for pair	$2,400	$2,900	10	10	10	30
* 3. Blondie's Jalopy in Marx box	$2,400	$2,900	10	10	10	30
4. Blondie 1938 press kit, inserts, mint (beautiful deco imagery)	$500	$2,000	10	10	10	30
** 5. Blondie 1934 Comic Construction Set in great deco-ish box	$350	$650	10	10	10	30
6. "Blondie Brings Up Baby" 1-sheet, 1939, unused mint	$400	$500	9.5	10	9	28.5
7. Blondie Cookbook, shadow-boxed, full-color 1940 print offer	$320	$500	10	10	8.5	28.5

Item	1999	2004	CF	SF	IF	TF
8. "Blondie has Servant Trouble" 1-sheet, unused mint (a bargain)	$175	$500	10	9	9.5	28.5
9. Blondie cookie cutters in box	$175	$250	9	9.5	9.5	28
10. Blondie from A to Z, shadow-boxed, color print offer	$175	$350	9	9	10	28
11. Blondie paint set, 1940, unused in box	$150	$250	9.5	9	9	27.5
12. "Blondie Meet the Boss," 14 x 36-inch insert poster, mint ...	$150	$250	9	9	9	
13. Dagwood & Blondie Jugate pinback, heads turned toward each other	$150	$250	9	9	9	27
14. Blondie radio cast photo set in original mailer (Singleton, Lake, Peary and Stafford)	$125	$225	8	9	10	27
15. Dagwood/Blondie Comic Togs Jugate pinback, heads facing same direction........................	$100	$220	8	9	10	27
16. "Blondie Takes a Vacation," 11 x 14-inch duotone card......	$75	$125	8	7	9	24
17. Dagwood/Blondie Post tin rings in containers, pair	$75	$125	9	6	9	24
18. "Blondie Plays Cupid," 11 x 14-inch color card	$75	$125	9	8	7	24
19. Blondie Goes to Leisureland game, unpunched pieces, spinner, mailer......................	$40	$125	10	4	10	24
20. Dagwood/Blondie lead pencils with tin bands around top	$25	$45	8	5	8	21

* Several similar toys exist (like the Charlie McCarthy and Mortimer Snerd wind-up coupe), and these are bringing $3,000-$4,000 in the box. At such prices, however, their investibility if an iffy proposition.

** Look in the color section for both versions of this super Blondie goodie: the black and white construction set and the near identical "Blondie Peg Set" from 1934.

CF-Collectibility Factor; SF-Scarcity Factor; IF-Investibility Factor; TF-Total Factor

---

Blondie 1934 Comic Construction Set is on the rise.

You will triple your money with the Blondie Goes to Leisureland game.

6 Board Games

History: Board games have been around forever. *They are—hands down—the most undervalued, entry-level category in character collectibles.* Dealers and savvy buyers are just beginning to heat up this market; for the first time, we are seeing pricey sale and auction ads with games that were shelf-sitters at $40 each a couple of years ago. Oddly enough, the earlier items have yet to take off as mainstream collector treasures because the characters (such as Buster Brown and Tige) have lost their broad audience appeal. As the older collectors (you know who you are) pass on to that big Trekkie con in the sky, and the average hobbyist's idea of something nostalgic becomes a set of Might Morphin Ninja Power Weasels, the turn-of-the-century and early-1900s games will gravitate toward museums or game completists. The hottest board games will be those from characters from 1930-1969.

The Flash/Justice League of America game.

The Buzz: Grab all the low-price games from major characters that have a personal appeal to you. If you can find any of these low priced and perfect, buy them: Buck Rogers, Gracie Allen, Philco Vance (version with metal playing pieces), both Superman games from the 1940s, The Shadow (the king of board games), Tarzan from the 1930s, Terry & the Pirates and The Green Hornet Secret Switch Game (still sealed).

Buy it now: If you can find virtually any major character board game with the playing pieces and/or accessories unpunched and sealed in the box, get it. (See "Amazing Spider-Man," for example). A sealed The Shadow boxed game sold for more than $2.000, and it will be double that by the time you're reading this. How many sealed 1940 *anything* could still exist from The Shadow?

Buy it later: Anything that isn't a must-have for your personal collection. Board games are still relatively easy to find, sealed items excluded, and there's no reason to succumb to bidding-war fever, especially for Western, general adventure and post-Boomer character games. Try to buy via direct sale ads or catalogs/lists, and buy from dealers who will guarantee condition and completeness after the sale.

Watch out: Stay away from taped or repainted boxes, unless it's a pre-1941 piece like Buck, Charlie Chan, Gracie Allen, Philco Vance, Tarzan, The Shadow or Superman. A rough corner or split box is preferable to mounds of tape or (horror of horrors) painted touch-ups. Fight the impulse to ever repair anything (unless you work for a restoration lab).

Rex Selections: Board Games

Item	1999	2004	CF	SF	IF	TF
1. Annie Oakley, 1964	$80	$120	9	8	8	25
2. Buck Rogers, 1934	$2,380	$3,500	10	10	10	30
3. Captain Gallant, 1965	$65	$90	6	7	6.5	19.5
4. Charlie Chan: Detective Mystery Game	$330	$450	10	9	8.7	27.7
* 5. Ellery Queen: Case of Elusive Assassin	$300	$450	9	9	10	28
6. Fireball XL-5, 1964 (a bargain)	$65	$110	10	7.5	10	27.5
7. The Flash/Justice League, 1967	$100	$250	10	8.5	10	28.5
8. Gang Busters, 1941	$85	$110	8	9	8	25
9. The Green Hornet Secret Switch Game, 1966, unused	$600	$900	10	8.5	10	28.5
10. Gunsmoke, 1958	$100	$130	10	8	9	27
11. Have Gun, Will Travel, 1959	$125	$175	10	9	10	29

Item	1999	2004	CF	SF	IF	TF
12. Hopalong Cassidy, 1950	$85	$130	10	8	10	28
13. Little Orphan Annie, 1927	$150	$190	8	10	7.5	25.5
14. Mandrake The Magician, 1966	$90	$175	9	8	8	25
15. Mighty Comics, 1966	$90	$130	9	7	7.5	23.5
16. Mighty Mouse, 1964	$60	$90	8.5	7	8.1	23.6
** 17. (The) Phantom: Ruler of the Jungle Game, 1966	$175	$375	10	9	10	29
*** 18. (The) Phantom, three game box, 1950s	$50	$75	8	6	8	22
19. Perry Mason, 1959	$70	$85	7	7	7	21
20. Philco Vance, non-metal version	$350	$425	10	10	8.5	28.5
**** 21. Philco/Gracie Allen Murder Case	$1,000	$1,250	10	10	9	29
22. Peter Gunn, 1960	$80	$95	7	7	7	21
***** 23. Superman, Adventures of, 1940	$330	$500	10	9.9	10	29.9
24. (The) Shadow, 1940	$700+	$1,000+	10	10	10	30
25. Star Trek, 1967	$185	$250+	10	7	8	25
26. Straight Arrow, 1950	$290	$450	10	9	10	29
27. Tarzan, skulls version, 1933-34	$450	$850	10	10	10	30
28. Wanted: Dead or Alive, 1959	$140	$250	9	9	9	27
29. Wonder Woman/Justice League, 1967	$170	$250	10	8	10	28

* Games like these, with plastic figurines, unused are sure bets. Also, see Ellery Queen in Chapter 22.

** The punch-out segment of this game, rather than the rinky-dink seal ring, is the most critical element to this game. The cardboard surround, which was intended to be discarded when the kid punched the board out, is the best part of the game's artwork.

*** A big hoard of these games were dumped on the market. The games are small and poorly designed. The Phantom's image appears about 11 times on the art; yet, it virtually feels as if it was an untied game. Pass.

**** This is a wonderful game based on the film from the Vance series, but it's already so costly the Investibility Factor is not quite a solid 30. Still, a great game.

***** See "Superman." A gum premium.

Mighty Comics Superheros is a great looking game, but ho-hum characters.

Game intelligence: Some auctioneers are selling the following items at ultra-high minimum-bid reserves, so if you must bid, do so cautiously. Here are prices from actual current catalogs, lists and ads. Mint condition is assumed. These are not what the games will sell for; this is the minimum they will permit one to bid. In many cases, the reserve is about a half or third of what the dealer feels the games will sell for. These sorts of minimum bids speak for themselves. Dealers believe they smell money! Happy hunting!

Batman, 1966	$150
Captain America, 1966	$125
Dick Tracy, 1933	$350 (!)
Dark Shadows, 1969	$290 (!)
Dragnet, 1955	$175 (!)
Hogan's Heroes, 1966	$100
The Rifleman, 1959 (what could they be thinking?)	$350 (!)
Sgt. Preston, 1955	$125
Superman Speed Game, 1940s	$175

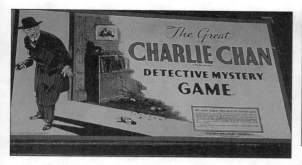

Charlie Chan: Detective Mystery Game is very hard to find.

Here's a best-bet—Terry and the Pirates box and board is a major bargain for $150 or less.

At $175, this killer board game from The Phantom is seldom found unpunched.

Mandrake The Magician game.

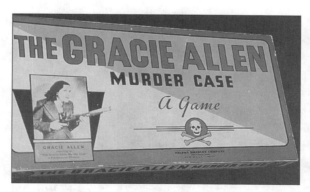

Philco/Gracie Allen Murder Case game is worth anything you have to pay under $1,000.

History: The Bowery Boys' origin was the stage play and the classic film, "Dead End." The boys had many incarnations as "The Dead End Kids," "The Little Tough Guys," "The East Side Kids" and combinations thereof. But they were referred to over the years as The Bowery Boys, and the name became official long after it had embedded itself in the public's mind around 1947. For two decades, they made picture after picture, sometimes together, sometimes as the primary stars (Frankie Darro, Leo Gorcey, Huntz Hall, William Benedict and others), worked by themselves or in tandem. The best movies were ones in which the chemistry between Gorcey and Hall was emphasized. By today's standards, the films might be deemed "unfunny," but they were enjoyable for the kids who grew up in the relatively innocent 1930s, 1940s and 1950s. These films played endlessly on TV and garnered a whole new audience of young fans.

The Buzz: Devoted Bowery Boys fans especially love paper from the so called "Old Dark House" or "sliding bookcase" movies which were perfect vehicles for the boys. Unlike memorabilia from The Three Stooges which has become high priced as to have no margin for investors, one can still find Bowery bargains in 1940s and 1950s signage. The first dark house picture the boys made was "Boys of the City" in 1940; and subsequent sliding bookcase titles are collectible, but the films themselves ("Bowery Boys Meet the Monsters") had become lame by the 1950s.

Buy it now: The pair of World War II pictures the boys did with Bela Lugosi (and a beautiful Ava Gardner, in one film), are only going to climb in value. Any premiums are also solid gold, if you can find them in the double-digit range.

Buy it later: Still photos, black-and-white lobbies and books about The Bowery Boys. Unusual black-and-white paper, such as framed promo ads or press kits, are okay.

Watch out: Don't buy any homages, pastiches, reproductions or tribute material with The Bowery Boys or any other character. It's 99% garbage.

Rex Selections: The Bowery Boys

Item	1999	2004	CF	SF	IF	TF
1. "Ghosts on the Loose" 1-sheet, unused	$475	$750	10	10	10	30
2. "Spooks Run Wild," color card with Lugosi, rare	$350	$550	10	10	10	30
3. "Spooks Busters" title card	$125	$175	9	8.5	9	26.5
4. Universal Serial pinbacks, each	$100	$150	9	10	7	26
5. "Ghost Chasers" 1-sheet	$100	$150	8	9	7	24

"Spooks Run Wild," color card with Lugosi.

History: Buck came from *Amazing Stories*, a so-called "bedsheet" (oversized) pulp magazine of the 1920s. The pulp was home for such classic authors as H.G. Wells. By the 1930s, the strip version of Buck, written by Phil Nowlan and drawn by Dick Calkins, was an absolute sensation. Although Buck Rogers is always lumped together with Flash Gordon, the similarities are superficial: They were space heroes with about the same balance of characters (a heroine, scientist, villain, etc.), but the look of the two strips was vastly different. Buck was comicy, a real Rube Goldberg-meets-Art Deco, as conceived by the brilliant Calkins, while Flash was done in a lush magazine "illustrator" style. Buck is by far the more collectible (serial paper excluded) because he was so heavily promoted with a remarkable array of toys, games, guns and gadgets. Buck was a big radio hit, unlike Flash who existed only in strip syndication form. Buck's premiums alone would keep a collector broke. We all want the same stuff—a pristine Adventure Book, mint-in-box ray guns and spaceships. What's not to love?

The Buzz: Today's hottest characters are Buck Rogers, Roy Rogers and Superman. As you'll learn in my chapter on Captain Marvel, there are characters with continuing marketplace "heat," but without sig-

nificant upward movement. With regard to the Investibility Factor, these have little room or margin for safe investment (save for items with unique pedigrees). Collectors are going to buy such pieces, but this is an *investor's guide* first, so the Collectibility Factor and Scarcity Factors are in place, but the Investibility Factor is iffy. Buck still has room to move, even at the current wildly inflated prices. It doesn't get much better than this: finding pristine or near flawless 1930s Buck stuff. Mint Buck Rogers memorabilia is as bankable as character collectibles get.

Buy it now: All of it, if you can find it and afford it. The one question I'm most often asked (besides land deed values) relates to the values and general investibility of Buck Rogers items: Why are his goodies bringing such high prices considering he was a Golden Age star? Won't prices drop when older collectors are replaced by post-Baby Boomers and Generation Xers who have forgotten Buck? Why do people pay big bucks for Buck? That's easy—look at the stuff. Does it get any cooler than a display of boxed ray guns or rocket ships? I don't think so. These are among the best designed toys and premiums ever. The Calkins' images translated perfectly into tin and cardboard, the blazing colors and strong deco lines were evocative of an entire time period. The young kids at the helm of big media outfits are all big sci-fi fans. They love rockets, robots and ray guns—all the top Buck, Flash and space

Set of six Big Thrill booklets, 1934, mint, $950.

Buck Rogers Atomic Pistol and holster set, will disintegrate your wallet at $3,000,

Buck Rogers Game of the 25th Century A.D. (listed under "Board Games"), $2,380.

goodies. They want it all mint in the box. You can't be too rich, too thin or have too many boxed Buck Rogers toys. God help you if you get into a bidding way with one of these young pups.

Buy it later: 1950s stuff. Concentrate on the gold.

Watch out: The 1933 map from Cocomalt, a killer premium, has been reproduced *and* faked, as have the painted lead figures. The fake isn't bad, but I don't buy this item anymore without the original mailing tube or unless the seller gives me a two-step provenance ("I got it from George who bought it from Joe whose father sent away for it and I'll give you a signed, notarized letter to that effect"). The 1932 "25th Century" Kellogg's book and the 1936 Disintegrator have been reproduced, but not faked,

as far as I know. The ray gun is completely different from the original. The fake map is like the fake Lone Ranger ring poster—too hard to differentiate by written description unless you have two examples—a real and a fake—to compare. By the way, when I refer to the fake Cocomalt map, I'm not talking about the laser photocopy, which is a different breed of weasel altogether.

Overview: If you're going to collect mint-in-box Roger items from the 1930s, you must be prepared to enter a super-hot, volatile seller's market. The world of pop culture collectibles is going to continue to become increasingly competitive as the supply of top condition merch dwindles, the demand grows and the X-Factor works its mysterious alchemy.

Rex Selections: Buck Rogers

Item	1999	2004	CF	SF	IF	TF
* 1. Deluxe Buck Rogers Scientific Laboratory	??	??	10+	10+	10+	40
2. Cut-Out Adventure Book, complete and uncut	$6,000	$10,000	10	10	10	30
** 3. Liquid Helium XZ-44 Water Pistol, red and yellow	$5,000	$10,000	10	11	10	31
4. Buck Rogers 1937 Battle of Mars Cannon with mint catalog	$4,000	$8,000	10	10	10	30
5. Buck Rogers 25th Century Rocket Ship, boxed, mint	$5,000	$6,000	10	10	10	30
6. Interplanetary Space Fleet Super-Dreadnaught, paints, original box	$4,000	$5,000	10	10	10	30
*** 7. Interplanetary Police Patrol keywind rocket ship in Marx box	$3,000	$4,000	10	10	10	30
8. Playsuit, complete with metal and leather helmet	$3,000	$4,000	10	10	10	30
**** 9. Buck Rogers Disintegrator from radio serial, 1930s	$3,000	$4,000	10	10	10	30
10. Atomic Pistol (any version in the yellow or red box)	$3,000	$4,000	10	10	10	30
11. Rocket Pistol (with holster) in box, 1934	$3,000	$4,000	10	10	10	30
12. Pocketwatch in box (provenance is important!)	$2,800	$3,800	10	10	10	30
13. Map of the Solar System in R.B. Davis tube (map alone)	$2,500	$3,500	10	10	10	30
14. Rocket Pistol (without holster) in box	$2,500	$3,500	10	10	10	30
15. Large version of 25th Century Chemical Lab in box	$2,000	$3,000	10	10	10	30
16. Buck Rogers Printing Set, complete in box	$1,000	$2,500	10	10	10	30
17. Buck Rogers Card Game in box	$1,000	$2,500	10	10	10	30
18. Projector with set of Buck Rogers rice paper cartoons in boxes	$1,000	$2,000	10	10	9	29
19. Set of six Big Thrill booklets, 1934, mint	$950	$2,000	10	10	9	29

Item	1999	2004	CF	SF	IF	TF
20. "I Saw Buck Rogers" World's Fair pinback, 1934	$950	$2,000	10	10	9	29
21. Rocket ship knife	$900	$2,000	10	10	9	29
22. Buck Rogers Solar Scouts 1936 manual in envelope	$900	$1,500	10	10	8	28
23. Buck Rogers 1941-42 Dog Tag with chain	$900	$1,500	10	10	8	28
24. Buck Rogers 1939 Strange World Adventures Club pinback/card.	$900	$1,250	10	10	7.5	27.5
25. Buck Rogers 1-sheet, restored	$900	$1,250	10	10	7	27

* This item does exist. At least one collector has a complete set with all the chemicals, telescope, manuals and so on. This is one of the two rarest boxed sets in character collecting, other than prototypes, and has no marketplace evaluation. It's likely worth $10,000 or more; $30,000-$50,000 in a bidding war.

** The red and yellow version with its lightning-bolt graphics and deco lines is far more collectible than the scarce but humdrum copper-colored one. One example is known with the bladder intact and working. It was obtained from the Los Alamos auction of ray guns and holsters from the Daisy Group.

*** #3 and #7 tailfins must be original.

**** I've never found the boxed version of this toy in presentable shape. The radio offer is copper colored, and various models were reissued throughout the post-war 1940s. The boxes, however, do not compare with those from the 1930s.

Final comments: I find that the Buck Rogers rings are very overpriced. Two have been faked and several Saturn Repeller Ray Rings were found without the small beveled green stone in them and beads were crafted to replace this element. A piece that I have no personal knowledge on is the set of three Tootsietoy ships: the Flash Blast Attack Ship, Venus Duo-Destroyer and the Battle Cruiser. I saw a man with the back seat of his car packed wall-to-wall with boxed ships. A hoard or...who knows? They looked all right to me, but the price was a grand for a set of three so I passed. He also had some boxed zeppelins. Perfect repros? I'm clueless. A 1930s Popsicle Buck Rogers store sign for the radio show was found in quantity; many were sold for $50 each. A recent auction hammered one down for more than $1,400.

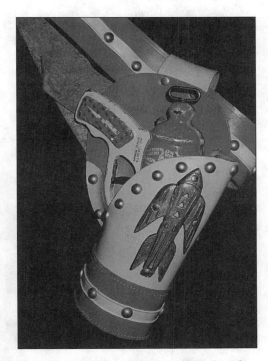

This Liquid Helium XZ-44 Water Pistol with 80% of it original paint is shown in a holster that was probably not Buck Rogers, but the metalwork includes a likeness similar to one of Buck's ships, and the water pistol displays nicely in it. The belt is from origins unknown, but valued at $1,000.

Liquid Helium XZ-44 Water Pistol, red and yellow; this is the only example with original bladder intact and working. The value is $5,000 or more.

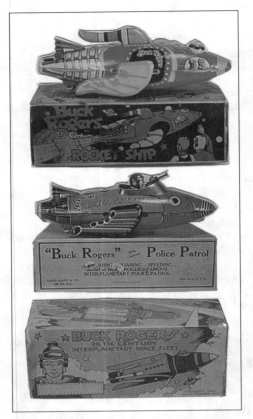

From top: Buck Rogers 25th Century
Rocket Ship, Police Patrol and Interplan-
etary Space Fleet Super-Dreadnaught the
paints are $4,000, $3,000 and $4,000,
respectively.

The Buck Rogers Rocket Pistol (without holster), mint in mint box is worth $2,500. One
in this condition is valued at $750.

Map of the Solar System with tube, illustrated letter and
adventure book has a current value of $6,000, with an
expected value of $10,000 by 2003. With emblem (not
shown), this set is valued currently at $8,000.

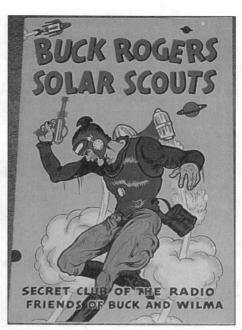

Buck Rogers Solar Scouts 1936 manual with envelope, $900.

This Buck Rogers Disintegrator ray gun from the radio serial, 1930s, has a value of $3,000 today, $4,000 probable by 2003.

Buck Rogers 1937 Battle of Mars Cannon with mint catalog has a value of $4,000.

Bugs Bunny

History: Bug's first incarnation was that of a mean-looking wabbit in Vitaphone's color cartoons. I'm so old I can remember selling a major comic book collector a VG copy of Looney Tunes & Merrie Melodies #1 for about $60, back when the 1941 first issues sold for chump change. It's obvious I was the "chump." Bugs and I are about the same age in bunny years, but he's old now and I'm still 11.

Buy it now: Vintage cartoon sheets are aimed skyward. Get what you can, while you can, if you can.

Buy it later: Pinbacks, postcards, popcorn boxes.

Watch out: Cels and pre-lims are pricey.

Rex Selections: Bugs Bunny

Item	1999	2004	CF	SF	IF	TF
1. Bugs Bunny cartoon poster, 1941	$1,500	$2,500	10	10	10	30
2. Bugs stock sheet poster without insert, 1946	$500	$800	10	10	9	29
3. Bugs alarm clock with animated carrot, in box	$500	$750	10	10	9	29
4. Bugs Bunny cast iron or pot metal bank	$240	$400	10	9	9	28
5. Bugs subscription portrait in mailer, 1946	$175	$300	9	8	9	26
6. Bugs Bunny, lot of three very mintish BLBs from the 1940s	$175	$250	8	8.5	9	25.5
7. Bugs Bunny Superstar Sign, heavy fiberboard	$170	$250	8	8	9.5	25.5
8. Bugs Bunny set of four 1940s mini comics with offer/mailer	$170	$225	9	9	7.5	25.5
9. Bugs Bunny rubber statuette	$100	$150	8	9	8	25
10. Bugs Bunny Movie Club Card, unused	$95	$150	8	9	8	25

This Bugs Bunny cartoon poster from 1941 has a predicted valued of $2,500 by 2004.

Bugs Bunny Superstar Sign, heavy fiberboard.

10 *Bulldog Drummond*

History: Bulldog Drummond is a character that generated little memorabilia, is highly investible, but the Scarcity Factor makes acquisitions challenging. First edition books with dust jackets are difficult to find. Movie paper, beginning with six and seven silent-reelers back in the 1920s, and select titles from two-dozen features such as the 1930s films in which—notoriously—John Barrymore appeared, is in demand. The radio series was tremendously popular in its day, but in three decades I have found one premium—a Sam Gold-designed Bulldog Drummond bomber put out by Horton around 1943. The market is too small to forecast a 2004 projection.

This Bulldog Drummond lobby card is valued at $150.

This Bulldog Drummond Bomber from Horton is priced at $350, with original mailer.

History: Synonymous with World War II, Captain America (and more recently Spy Smasher), was the "other" superhero of the 1940s to catch fire. The late Phil Seuling's advice to me when I first began buying comics in the 1960s included this word on Captain America titles: "Stay away from these books until you've done your homework." The master dealer's words still ring true. Excluding, perhaps, movie paper from the original release of the serial, comics have little margin for investibility for the average collector of character items and no room for mistakes. Multiply that by 10 for original art.

The Buzz: You are in heated competition with thousands of both average and well-healed superhero collectors when you vie for Captain America items. An illustrated, empty mailing envelope sold for $1,000. There are two Sentinels of Liberty cards and two original premium shields, which are four of the most sought collectibles around.

Buy it now: If you can find anything like the 1941 premium kits or a damaged (coverless, water-stained…"worthless") comic such as "All Winners #10" that has a frameable shield offer or any Captain America full-page ad, try to buy them. Have the ad matted and framed and take it to the bank. Look for serial paper, too.

Buy it later: Any serial re-release, however pretty.

Watch out: Remember this rule of thumb: If it can be faked, it probably has been. Fair warning. The *reproduction* of the Captain America shield has been faked! The reverse marking has been obliterated and the obverse has been artificially aged. On the *new* shield, the "E" in America is centered under the "P" of Captain, but not the 1941 original shield.

Rex Selections: Captain America

Item	1999	2004	CF	SF	IF	TF
* 1. Captain America Serial valance	$5,000	$11,000	10	10	10	30
2. Captain America Sentinels of Liberty Pledge to Principles and Official Membership Card (aquamarine, red and white)	$2,000	$3,000	10	10	10	30
3. Captain America Sentinels of Liberty Pledge to Principles and Official Membership Card (dark blue, red and white)	$2,000	$3,000	10	10	10	30
4. Copper Sentinels of Liberty Shield	$3,000	$5,000	10	10	10	30
5. Brass Sentinels of Liberty Shield	$2,500	$4,500	10	10	10	30

* This is a fabric banner with a World War II/factory tie-in.

1941   Repro

On the left is the original 1941 Sentinels of Liberty Shield, and on the right is the reproduced version. Note the alignment of the "P" in Captain and the "E" in America. Don't get burned on a repro.

History: Billy Batson would speak the magic word and turn into Captain Marvel. He came along in 1940, drawn in the somehow primitive and wonderful comic book style of C.C. Beck. For much of the Golden Age, Captain Marvel rivaled Superman as a comic star. From his print origin in an "ash can" comic (the first Whiz was actually numbered #2, a kind of homage to Captain Billy's Whiz-Bang of old), a treasure trove of paper and, less frequently, hardware items were brought out by the people at Fawcet. The first item was a whistle called the "Power Siren," and a store display of mint ones is probably the most desired Captain Marvel piece under $5,000 (see "Original Art" chapter).

The Buzz: It is now very difficult to buy Captain Marvel's best memorabilia with an eye toward potential appreciation (two boxed Captain Marvel puzzles in mint just sold for $2,500—well beyond their worth, in my opinion). Avid fans of The Big Red Cheese conspire to price the real goodies to the max and beyond. Example: The least expensive of the various 1940s painted statuettes is already selling for more than $5,000. An advanced collector estimate a set of Kerr Company statuettes is valued at "over $25,000, conservatively." Aside from some of the old radio comedians, whose mint boxed tin toys have shot into the five-figure range, Captain Marvel is one of the only major characters who is hot, but has relatively low investibility for most hobbyists.

Buy it now and buy an extra for me: A world War II pressed-wood statuette, a set of 1947 race cars with keys in a complete box, a Dell Fast Action Book in perfect shape and an art deco compass ring *in the mailer with paperwork.*

Rex Selections: Captain Marvel

Item	1999	2004	CF	SF	IF	TF
1. Power Siren display with 12 sirens, 1940	$3,750	$5,500	10	10	10	30
* 2. "Adventures of Captain Marvel" 3-sheet, 1941	$4,500	$6,500	10	10	10	30
3. Set of three unused coloring and paint books, 1940s	$2,500	$3,500	10	10	10	30
4. E-Z Code Finder with mailer and Captain Marvel Adventures	$2,500	$3,500	10	10	10	30
5. Captain Marvel 1946 cap or Shazam Club beanie, complete with set of dime-size pinbacks (10) mounted on cap	$1,500	$2,000	10	10	10	30
** 6. Captain Marvel 1948 shirt or sweatshirt with large pin	$1,500	$2,000	10	10	10	30
7. Captain Marvel 1946 Adventures in Paint set	$1,000	$1,500	10	10	10	30
** 8. Captain Marvel 1948 wristwatch with insert	$900	$1,200	10	9.5	9.9	29.4
9. Basic six-part Shazam 1940s Membership Kit	$750	$1,000	10	9	9	28
10. Captain Marvel 1944 Magic Lightning Box	$250	$350	10	9	8	27

The combination of a major character and unique item or pedigree equals solid-gold investibility. "Captain Marvel Adventures" were taped at each corner to Wheaties cereal boxes. Offered in 1945, they were promoted in comic strip ads and over the Jack Armstrong and Lone Ranger radio programs. A total of one high-grade file copy is known to exist. The extraordinary book has never been taped and is an extremely rare collectible. The Overstreet guide doesn't even list a value for a copy of this comic without tape! This unique example is in near-original condition and valued at $20,000, and its future is well over $30,000, since it is the rarest surviving Captain Marvel premium.

* Serial 3-sheets are very difficult to evaluate because of the wide price swings. Unlike 41 x 27-inch 1-sheet posters, serial 3-sheets (which range 80-82 inches x 40-41 inches, and were made from pieces that were assembled by the exhibitor) are becoming tough to find, especially in top grade. Current ranges for the above 3-sheet are $4,500-$7,500, with a potential of $6,500-$9,500 by 2004.

** Needs to have original foil and other inserts.

E-Z Code Finder with print ad from Captain Marvel Adventures #25.

Captain Marvel 1944 Magic Lightning Box

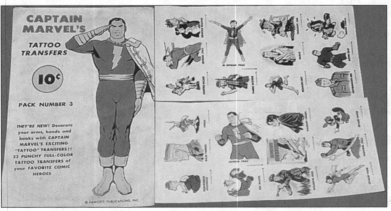

These Captain Marvel Tattoo Transfers is a World War II-era item valued at $275.

Captain Marvel 1946 Adventures in Paint set will set you back a cool grand.

The inside of the Adventures in Paint set.

Captain Marvel 1948 wristwatch in original box.

History: Midnight followed Jimmie Allen on 1930s radio and in the comic strips, another of the many aviation heroes created for the air and print by the Bertt-Moore writing team. There were several Midnight personas: 1) the radio Midnight whose stream of decoders, manuals and Secret Squadron rings echoed the success of radio's Little Orphan Annie, and kept Ovaltine a household word from 1940-1950; 2) the comics Midnight, which ranged from early Raboy art to some lackluster post-war images in which Fawcett presented him as a kind of para-winged quasi-superhero; 3) the serial star of war time years; 4) and the clean-cut TV aviator portrayed by my friend of bygone days, Dick Webb. Each Captain Midnight is associated with a wealth of collectible byproducts.

The Buzz: The character is much beloved by premium buffs. Radio-era gold ranges from a small $12 Skelly coin to a huge wooden Skelly sign that surfaces now and again, usually overpriced. Every old kid who recalled listening to this old serial has a false memory of a decoder ring. There were decoders and rings, but the closest artifact with a decoding/deciphering aspect is the Flight Commander's ring with a secret number inside; yet we all have this collective image in our heads of a premium that never existed.

Buy it now: The Captain Midnight Mystic Sun-God Ring, still the standard for exquisite sendaways, has yet to "go platinum," as it were. Buy pristine mint, and if you can find it in a mailer with the little manual, so much the better. One version, incidentally, came with a small two-tone blue prize card from the good Captain.

Buy it later: Personally, I have never had either of the two large cardboard display signs, and I doubt if I'll ever find them at a reasonable price. I wouldn't worry about picking up secondary stuff, however rare, unless you feel it's bargain priced. Newsletters and off-beat maps, the rare but nondescript Skelly badges, balsa airplane kits, unmarked ribbons, TV-

Dick Webb as Captain Midnight.

era insignia patches…they can wait. Concentrate on the decoders, manuals, rings, Detect-O-Scope and Spy Scope, Shake-Up Mugs and the rare chapter play standee.

Watch out: There's a great deal of stuff to be had from other countries, such as Australia and Great Britain, ranging from a full run of comic books and art to a small statuette. Most of these things don't have much future collectibility, outside the small market of hard-core completists.

Rex Selections: Captain Midnight

Item	1999	2004	CF	SF	IF	TF
* 1. Complete set of Secret Decoders and Secret Manuals	$35,000	$70,000	10	10	10	30
** 2. Captain Midnight Mystic Sun-God Ring	$4,750+	$10,000	10	10	10	30
3. Captain Midnight Flight Patrol Map, matted and framed	$1,500	$3,000	10	10	10	30
4. MJC-10 Plane Detector with inserts, uncut instructions, mailer.	$1,250	$2,700	10	10	10	30
5. Captain Midnight Flight Commander WWII "Super Code" Ring, uncirculated proof mint	$1,250	$2,500	10	10	10	30
6. Ovaltine Flight Commander Badge	$750	$1,250	10	10	10	30
7. WWII Magic Black-Out Lite-Ups	$650	$850	9	9	10	28
8. 1947 unpainted P.A.P. Statuette	$400	$750	9	10	9	28
9. Sleeve insignia with color folder	$350	$500	9	9	8	26
10. Captain Might Detect-O-Scope, metal gauge and instructions	$350	$500	10	9	8	27

* A complete set of Secret Decoders (cipher discs) and Secret Manuals is worth far more as a lot than the sum of the parts. Begin picking up all the decoding hardware from radio shows such as Midnight, Annie, Tom Mix, Sky King, etc., A set with the manuals or instruction sheets sold for $35,000 with all of these items in pristine mint condition. The set should be worth about twice that in 2004. Broken up, solid at matching units, it would not be nearly as valuable, which reverses the traditional antique dealer's theory about liquidation.

** This is a gorgeous artifact; several uncirculated proof-mint examples were found back in the early-1970s, in the Robbins Company trove.

This Captain Midnight Flight Patrol Map has a $1,500 value.

This is part of the $35,000 of Captain Midnight decoders.

Captain Midnight Flight Commander WWII "Super Code" Ring.

Ovaltine Flight Commander Badge.

In pristine uncut condition with the mailer, this MJC-10 Plane Detector sells for a lofty $1,250.

Sleeve insignia with color folder.

44

Cereal Boxes

History: The milling companies began using characters heavily with the advent of the kids' serials of the early-1930s. Some were product-driven, like Inspector Post, while others, such as Skippy, used the character to move the product. In the mid-1950s, with the strength of the new baby-sitter (TV), the cereal companies charged full-tilt ahead into TV with cardboard guns, figurines, toys, games, comics and decoder items. Boomers get into the later stuff, but, viewed objectively, the post-1950s cereal boxes never had the muscle of the older pieces.

The Buzz: The mid-1960s is the hot cereal box time, but I don't see much margin left there. There are *astronomical* prices being paid today for boxes from tele-characters such as the Beverly Hillbillies. I'm talking thousands of dollars; it's difficult to see room for investibility. People start quoting $5,000 price tags for Quisp and Quake and I just get sleepy. Do you know what I mean? Sorry…I can't help you on this one.

Buy it now: The Golden Age boxes seem dramatically undervalued, as the wildly publicized modern-day boxes rocket out of site.

Rex Selections: Cereal Boxes

Item	1999	2004	CF	SF	IF	TF
* 1. The Lone Ranger Frontier Town, 1948, four sendaway sections and nine Cheerios boxes, as a complete lot	$8,000	$10,500	10	10	10	30
2. Sgt. Preston Yukon Trail, 1950, set of four	$2,500	$3,500	10	9.5	10	29.5
3. Buck Rogers Post Toasties Ring box, 1946.	$750	$1,000	10	10	10	30
* 4. Jack Armstrong Phantom Sub Hide-Out Offer	$500	$750	10	10	9	29
5. Superman Kellogg's Pep Pins and Beanie box	$450	$700	10	9	10	29
6. Terry & the Pirates Wings of Victory box, 1943	$450	$675	10	10	9	29
7. Dick Tracy Secret Service Patrol Quaker's box, 1938	$450	$650	10	10	9	29
8. Donald Duck mini-comics offer	$450	$650	10	10	9	29
9. Mickey Mouse cut-outs offer, 1930s	$450	$675	10	10	10	30
10. Sgt. Preston Canoe Race box offer	$150	$250	9	8	9	26

* #3 from 1930s set of six boxes is especially sought.

Half of the Green Hornet Model City is shown. The premium never caught on because collectors generally refused to believe it's tied to the character. It was offered in "Green Hornet Fights Crime #36." The six trays have a $900 value, with the offer illustrated with the Green Hornet's image. It's a tough sell!

The 1948 Lone Ranger Frontier Town box front, back and 25% of the sendaway sections, with the ground plan in mailer. The complete set of four boxes is valued at $8,000.

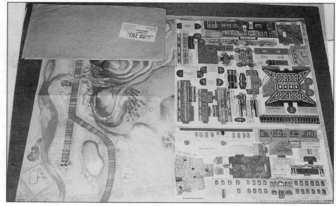

This set of 1950 Sgt. Preston Yukon Trail boxes from Quaker Puffed Wheat is valued at $2,500

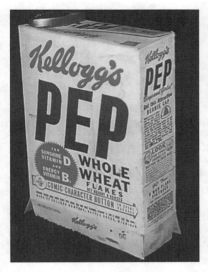

Superman Kellogg's Pep Pins and Beanie box looks like a bargain at $450.

From the sideview, you can see the front and back of the Terry & the Pirates Wings of Victory box, which is priced at $450 now.

Jack Armstrong Phantom Sub Hide-Out Offer from Wheaties is a $500 box.

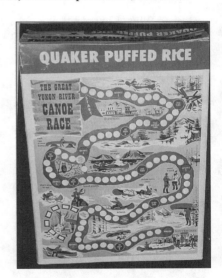

Sgt. Preston Canoe Race box is currently valued at $150.

Can you spot the hot box? Winnie the Pooh fans will. The Pooh box is a $65 bargain!

History: Chandu the Magician was a creature of the early-1930s, who came alive with the obsolescence of messy battery radio sets and the primitive crystal receivers of the 1920s. Networks and syndicators suddenly were looking for adventure shows to placate the big-time sponsors coming over from print. Chandu was created just for such a need; by 1932. He was—excuse the expression—bicoastal. His corporate sponsors (White King Granulated Soap and Beech-Nut Gum) flogged the airwaves with sendaway offers for magical premiums. Chandu, a tremendous hit, was the star of his own Principal chapter play by 1934. It starred Bela Lugosi, fresh from such major pictures as "Dracula," cast as eerie good guy Frank Chandler.

Buy it now: The deluxe Chandu White King of Magic Trick Set was $2 or a stack of soap labels back in 1932; it could cost you up to $500 today, mint with manual, but it's a stone killer. An interesting Beech-Nut Svengali Mind-Reading Trick is one of the only known premiums made in the likeness of the radio sponsor's product.

Buy it later: Individual tricks other than those previously mentioned.

Rex Selections: Chandu

Item	1999	2004	CF	SF	IF	TF
1. Chandu White King of Magic Trick Set	$500	$750	9	9	9	27
2. Chandu Chapter Play Mask (two different ones available), each	$300	$450	9	10	8	27
3. Chandu Svengali Mind-Reading Trick, boxed, with instructions	$125	$150	10	9	7.5	26.5
4. Chandu (Frank Chandler and cast) Mystic Crystal Photo	$100	$125	10	10	6	26
* 5. Lobby cards from Chandu serial and edited features	$50+	$100+	10	9	7	26

* "Chandu on the Magic Island," a.k.a., "Magic Isle," is one of the two or three serial edits that retained the power of the original work. This is no small achievement.

You have to pay $500 or more for the Chandu White King of Magic Trick Set.

This lobby card from a Chandu serial is valued at $50-$100.

History: Earl Derr Biggers, the author of such early-1900s mysteries as *Seven Keys to Baldpate*, created his corpulent Honolulu cop for *The House Without a Key* in 1925. Chan went on to star in silent movies, hardcover and paperback novels, vintage radio, early TV and in what seemed like an endless series of films that were still strip-programmed as late nighttime fillers in the 1950s. Performer Steve Allen told me that he knew the concept of the late-night talk show would work because—in his words—by 1953, "people were sick and tired of watching Charlie Chan movies on The Late, Late Show." Few sleuths have been as durable or as poorly marketed as Charlie Chan.

The Buzz: Rare first editions of *The House Without a Key*, *Behind That Curtain* (1928), *The Black Camel* (1929) and *Charlie Chan Carries On* (1930) are very difficult to find with the dust jackets. Reprints and paperbacks are relatively worthless. Silent movie and pre-war Chan paper is smokin' hot. Post-war cools down in price, but there's a modest investibility margin.

Buy it now: Strip runs— Alfred Andriola was a killer artist on this title; original art, Andriola personal items related to the characters, mint BLBs, 1930s Warner Oland posters (if you can afford them), board games, card games, the Topps Gum Flip-O-Vision card set (if you can find it), photos from the Chan radio show, heralds, handbills…all the unusual pieces.

Buy it later: Don't overpay through an auction or rare bookseller for hardcovers without dust jackets.

Used book stores sometimes have these dust jacketless books at bargain prices.

Watch out: Don't get stung on a sky-high priced silent sheet, thinking you have found a major Charlie Chan collectible. Chan was a peripheral character in such early titles as the 1926 chapter play version of the first story, "Behind That Curtain"; the first Charlie Chan talkie released in 1929; and the first Chan that videophiles have found is essentially a Warner Baxter movie, with the Honolulu sleuth in a minor role, played by unknown E.L. Park in the part.

At left is the Charlie Chan Card Game ($190) and at right is the Charlie Chan BLB ($75). Both share the same artwork of Alfred Andriola.

Rex Selections: Charlie Chan

Item	1999	2004	CF	SF	IF	TF
1. "Charlie Chan Carries On," 1931, 1-sheet	$1,800	$2,500	10	10	10	30
2. "The Black Camel," 1931, 1-sheet	$1,750	$2,500	10	10	10	30
3. "Charlie Chan's Greatest Case," 1933, 1-sheet	$1,650	$2,300	10	10	10	30
4. "Charlie Chan's Courage," 1934, 1-sheet	$1,500	$2,200	10	10	10	30
5. "Charlie Chan in London," 1934, 1-sheet	$1,500	$2,200	10	10	10	30
6. "Charlie Chan in Paris," 1934, 1-sheet	$1,500	$2,500	10	10	10	30
* 7. "Charlie Chan in Egypt," 1935, 1-sheet	$1,500	$2,500	10	10	10	30
** 8. Charlie Chan poster lot of four titles	$8,000	$12,000	10	10	10	30
*** 9. Charlie Chan Flip-O-Vision set	$350	$550	10	10	10	30
**** 10. Charlie Chan Card Game	$190	$350	10	9.5	10	29.5

* With the beautiful Rita Hayworth when she was still Rita Casino.

** A lot of four titles—"Charlie Chan at the Circus" (1936), "Charlie Chan at the Racetrack" (1936), "Charlie Chan in Honolulu" (1938) and "Charlie Chan at Treasure Island" (1939)—brought $8,000 at auction. No one seemed to feel the price was excessive for those high-profile titles, three of which were in top grade. Other important and pricey sheets include "Charlie Chan at the Opera" (1936) and a less-rare favorite "Charlie Chan at the Wax Museum." In a sleeper, try to get lobby cards or anything you can from "Charlie Chan in Black Magic" in the 1944 release before it was retitled. ("Murder at Midnight," the only Chan allowed to fall into Public Domain, was deemed politically incorrect in the raised consciousness of the 1950s.) You can sometimes find color cards from this title for well under $200, and they are a $400 goodie for the future.

*** Only one known Chan premium was issued in the Golden Age, a remarkable fact given the popularity of the character. I know of no tin toys, store displays or radio sendaways, save for an Esso Oil photograph. The Topps Gum folks issued a set of 30 gum cards in 1949 made from still frames of Chan with a magnifying lens and promoting the movie "Charlie Chan in Sky Dragon." These worked like BLB flipbooks: The cards could be collected, collated in order, then held together at the bottom notches by a rubber band or piece of string When flipped, the cards created a sense of movement. The rarity of such a piece is self-evident.

**** This neat boxed item has a cover that uses Alfred Andriola art, as does one of the Chan BLBs. Other than original artwork and personalized Chan notes from Andriola to friends or fans, I've encountered to off-beat collectibles for this major name. Also, see "Board Games" chapter.

> **CF-Collectibility Factor; SF-Scarcity Factor;**
> **IF-Investibility Factor; TF-Total Factor**

The complete set of Charlie Chan Flip-O-Vision cards is valued at $350 today, projected at $550 by 2004.

History: It always amazed me that a dummy and a ventriloquist (and one who moved his mouth—Edgar Bergen even kidded about his ineptitude, all the way to the bank) could become of the most popular "characters" of all time. Think about the concept: a radio ventriloquist! It makes as much sense as a magician on the radio. But we *believed* back then, and Bergen's sense of character was every bit as vital as Jack Benny or W.C. Fields'. Their sponsorship alliance with Chase & Sanborn Coffee was one of the strongest of the 1930s.

The Buzz: If you want to collect keywind toys and you have the cash, you might consider picking up a few of the mint and boxed toys from radio comedians of the 1930s. Start with Charlie; if you have any money left, you could move on to Amos 'n' Andy. The stuff not only seems to have no investibility margin, it appears to have gone totally bonkers. Wanna go $11,000 for a Charlie and Mortimer Coupe? Me, neither.

Buy it now: Virtually any of the radio-era memorabilia is worth getting. Even commonplace pieces, such as the Radio Party Game, a sendaway issued in ultra-high numbers back in the 1930s, are charming display pieces that you can buy very reasonably and resell, if need be, at a profit. Marx issued several keywind Charlie McCarthy cars and figures, but they all seem to lack investor potential. For example, the keywind Charlie McCarthy/Mortimer Snerd Coupe ("We'll Mow You Down") which was issued about the time Bergen brought Snerd into the radio fold in 1939, just sold for around $10,000. It's a solid 30, but there's no way for me to project prices for such merchandise. Who would have thought that comics would be selling in six-figures? I doubt even Overstreet himself could have called that one when he put out his first price guide. The only thing we can count on with regards to the Charlie McCarthy cars and figures is that they are going up in price.

Charlie cardboard dummy in mailer is a $200 item.

Buy it later: 1950s comic books appear to have temporarily stiffed-out. Pass on Coke signs and Mazuma Funny Money.

Watch out: Never buy anything that's been repainted. Collectors and dealers seem compelled to "improve" the details of the crude but cute carnival dolls we used to refer to as kewpies ("kewpies" spelled in lowercase to differentiate from Rose O'Neill figures). These pieces are not so rare that you have to buy repaired or repainted figures.

Rex Selections: Charlie McCarthy

Item	1999	2004	CF	SF	IF	TF
1. Charlie McCarthy alarm clock	$1,750	$2,500	10	10	10	30
2. "Charlie McCarthy, Detective" 1-sheet	$1,200	$1,700	10	10	10	30
3. Charlie McCarthy figural brass ring (only buy in near mint-plus)	$600	$850	10	10	10	30

Item	1999	2004	CF	SF	IF	TF
* 4. Charlie McCarthy Ventriloquist Dolls, clothed	$675	$850	10	10	10	30
5. "Hello Pal," short story, comics, McCarthy issue	$300	$500	10	10	10	30
6. Edgar Bergen/Charlie McCarthy Scrap Drive Sign.	$250	$450	10	10	10	30
7. Charlie cardboard dummy in mailer	$200	$300	10	9	9	28
8. Charlie McCarthy pencil sharpener in mailer	$175	$225	10	9	8	27
9. Charlie McCarthy carnival statue, original paint and glitter . . .	$100	$150	9	9	8	26
10. Charlie McCarthy Radio Party in mailer.	$75	$150	10	8	8	26
11. Charlie McCarthy/Sherlock Holmes Detective Spoon	$75	$150	10	9	8	27

* Believe it or not, they still sell Charlie McCarthy dummies in contemporary toy stores.

This is a rare "Charlie McCarthy, Detective" two-page color promo valued at $125 unframed.

Charlie's "Benzine Buggy" is worth big bucks in the box.

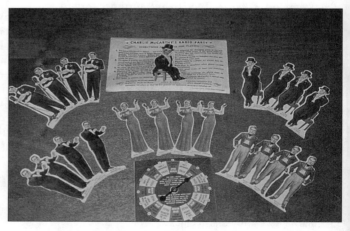

Charlie McCarthy Radio Party in mailer is a solid buy at $75.

History: Between 1931 (the inception of the lantern-jawed copper who first called "Plainclothes Tracy" by his creator Chester Gould) and 1977 (when Gould retired), it would probably not be an exaggeration to say that 10,000 collectibles were produced in one form or another. In addition to the comic strips, there were Dick Tracy books and magazines, a vast array of toys, premiums, film, tape and record items, store pieces by the bucketful, and on and on. Tracy's adventures live on in four chapter plays, five feature films, live and animated TV...every venue available.

The Buzz: Tracy was the ultimate in violence, as family strips went back in the 1940s, so toy guns are always evocative to collect. The 1946 metal Tommy Gun from Parker-Johns is a particularly well-made toy. Everybody loves wrist radios; they were created in 1946, and working models sold through 1947 comic books like "Zoot" are among the most hunted of all sendaways. It took a pair to make them work, and one of mine still has a functioning diode, amazingly. A pair will bring high four-figures, as will any of the store displays, 1937 serial posters or pieces such as the wooden carnival flat joint, big pedal car with figures or unique theatrical exhibitor's promo pieces.

Buy it now: Buy all the Secret Service Patrol shields: Half a dozen of these in pristine condition, shadow-boxed with either a Tracy Quaker's box or 1938 Promotional Record will cost you $1,500-$2,000, if you pick them up carefully, and you'll have yourself a $4,000 collection when the smoke clears (the I.G. shield is generally overpriced). Tracy jugates are golden.

This is the real deal! A pair of Dick Tracy Wrist Radios from Damyco, boxed, with all the goodies and in working condition, sell for $9,000 today.

Buy it later: "Dick Tracy Detective" pinbacks, Crime Detection Folios, Crime Stopper Kits or Remco Wrist Radios.

Watch out: Hot-iron "Dick Tracy Crimestopper" transfers seem super-abundant.

Rex Selections: Dick Tracy

Item	1999	2004	CF	SF	IF	TF
* 1. Dick Tracy Wrist Radios, Damyco, boxed, for pair	$9,000	$12,000+	10	10	10	30
** 2. "Dick Tracy," chapter play, 3-sheet, 1937	$8,000	$11,000	10	10	10	30
3. Dick Tracy Electric Rapid-Fire Tommy Gun, metal, boxed, 1947	$3,000	$4,000	10	10	10	30
*** 4. Sweet Company store display for Dick Tracy Kit, 1945	$2,750	$3,750	10	10	10	30
5. Dick Tracy Miller Bros. Hats, diecut display with brown or blue hat	$2,500	$3,200	10	9.9	10	29.9

Item	1999	2004	CF	SF	IF	TF
6. Dick Tracy store ad, plus Comic Ring (Gold Archives) in wrapper and 1940s Post Raisin Bran cereal box	$2,500	$3,500	10	9.9	10	29.9
7. Dick Tracy 1930s Gould Art—Tommy Gun scene	$2,500	$3,250	10	10	9.9	29.9
8. Dick Tracy 1940s Gould Art—Sparkle Cola scene	$2,200	$3,000	10	10	9.8	29.8
9. Dick Tracy Candy Offer, matted and framed	$1,000	$1,250	10	10	9	29
10. Dick Tracy, second version of Sweet Detective Set with "Air Aces" offer.	$900	$1,250	10	10	9	29

* For this price, the Wrist Radios must be boxed, with all accessories and illustrated instructions that depict Tracy with Billy Batson, the only such combination of these two characters that exists. This Wrist Radio came in yellow, black or red. A pair in pristine condition, with crystal diodes intact, represents one of the top-five comic character collectibles of all time. It is the ultimate, bar none. There were maybe a dozen variations on the wrist radio/TV theme, but only this one was offered as the premium that was once said to "both transmit and receive," just like Dick Tracy's own. It was the equivalent of having a live silver bullet from The Lone Ranger or a piece of *real* Kryptonite from Superman.

** None of the later sequels or features are this valuable. "Dick Tracy" 3-sheets from the post-war 1940s, as well as 1950s re-release posters, are commonplace.

*** Price for complete store display with World War II propaganda material.

Dick Tracy Miller Bros. blue hat, with the diecut display (not shown) is an item that sells for $2,500.

This is a Dick Tracy store ad for Comic Rings that were packaged in 1940s Post Raisin Bran cereal. (photo courtesy of Christie's East)

Dick Tracy Super Comics.

This Dick Tracy Target is valued at $75

History: Around 1929, when The Shadow first appeared as a relatively minor print character, a writer named Lester Dent began working for the famous pulp magazine publisher Street & Smith, which would first sponsor radio's "The Shadow" in 1930—as "Detective Story Hour"—and then begin a Shadow pulp magazine a year later. The Shadow was a different character in the pulps than he was on vintage air, but both print and radio versions became major success stories.

By 1933, Les Dent and the Street & Smith gang had refined and sculpted a character they knew had the legs to run on the same fast track as The Shadow. Doc Savage, "The Man of Bronze," an obvious borrow from Tarzan (The Bronzed-Light Ape Man), appeared in his first pulp magazine and, to match The Shadow, a set of three books with color hardcovers. Writing under the S&S house-name Kenneth Robeson, there would ultimately be 182 Doc Savage pulps, and Dent would pen most of them. Even L. Ron Hubbard, dog's years before *Dianetics*, worked on Doc Savage! A complete run of pulps sold for a staggering sum some years back, but a truckload of money probably couldn't buy a set today in original condition.

Doc Savage was a radio series that was broadcast in syndication briefly in 1934—two store signs and a set of scripts to attest. It first aired over 60 stations for a sponsor called Cystex. Another sign proclaimed, "You can now hear the adventures of Doc Savage and his pals on the air—more than 75 stations carry the Doc Savage programs."

By the time Doc was circulating over the airwaves, there was a mysterious radio program already on the air known as "The Avenger" (referred to as "The Weird Avenger" on premiums, brochures and early signage by both pulp magazine and radio people). The Avenger counter-programmed against The Shadow. No one knows for sure what The Avenger show was like, as no known recordings or scripts survive, but according to one sign found, the program had a sponsor—a heartland-based coffee company.

The original Avenger of the early-1930s is the real secret story. Ultimately, it would become a Les Dent pulp, and there would be comics planned and broadcast incarnations would come to life, but was the first

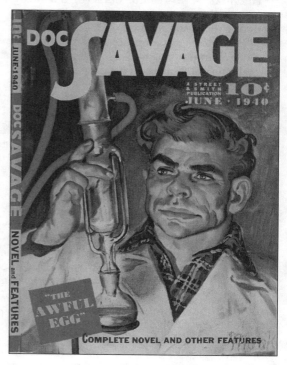

Doc Savage magazine from June 1940.

version of The Avenger radio broadcast a major influence for the characters that would evolve over time. Examples of this program would be immensely valuable and historically important to today's collectors of The Shadow, Doc Savage and The Avenger.

The Shadow was relentlessly imitated, and some of the print and broadcast clones were just plain embarrassing (they were so bad). One example, however, the pulp hero of the 1939-1941 period, was more than merely a pale imitation of The Shadow. Lester Dent's The Avenger was, as so many heroic images would be, a combination of many characters—some well known and other now obscure, like The Whisperer of the pulps.

Street & Smith also pubbed Doc Savage's exploits in some 30 comic books bearing Doc's name, and the character with "gold-flake eyes" appeared in most issues of Shadow Comics, both books beginning in 1940. Doc Savage never found his way to the movie serial screen, unfortunately, and "Doc Savage: The Man of Bronze," released in 1975, was uninspired. The movie should have worked; it was the great George Pal's last picture, but it came in the wake of the 1960s nostalgia craze, when such subject matter was deemed "high camp" and was treated accordingly.

The Buzz: A first-edition of the 1933 hardcover book with decent exterior and untouched interior pages or a top-grade condition "Doc Savage Magazine #1" is a four-star collectible in every way. Even the modestly priced color posters that reproduce the Walter Baumhofer cover art have great appeal.

Doc Savage and The Avenger memorabilia is hard to locate. Not even Dent himself had what could be called an extensive collection. He owned a Savage cover portrait, the run of magazines and was once "given a handful" of premium badges, cards, rubber stamps and the like while visiting the offices of the publishers. I was able to purchase a few items from the Dent estate.

Buy it now: *The Man of Bronze* hardcover in as mintish shape as the woodpeckers will allow. It's still affordable and reproduces the noteworthy Walter Baumhofer artwork from "Doc Savage Magazine #1" (fast becoming unfindable). Try to find the Doc Savage Award and Medallion, as well as The Avenger and Doc Savage radio signs, of which three are known. Transcriptions of The Avenger would find a ready market for the first entrepreneur who can turn up an example of this vintage 1930s radio program.

Buy it later: Heavily taped, ripped, stained pulp magazines; Doc Savage Club Badges if they are wildly overpriced; Club rubber stamps if not in mailers.

Doc Savage cards, rubber stamp, badge, medallion with papers, in mailer unused with signed estate (Les Dent) provenance on George Pal studio letterhead, valued at $20,000 and up!

The Avenger magazine from February 1940.

Rex Selections: Doc Savage

Item	1999	2004	CF	SF	IF	TF
1. Doc Savage Cards (two different), Rubber Stamp, Club Badge, Medallion, Papers, Application, all unused with signed estate of Lester Dent provenance on George Pal studio letterhead	$20,000+	$30,000+	11	11	11	33
2. Doc Savage #1 original art and color hardcover	$12,500	$15,000	11	11	10	32
* 3. Both Baumhofer Doc Savage portraits	$4,000	$6,000	11	10	10	31
4. Pair of Doc Savage program ads on cardboard, each	$1,200	$1,500	10	10	10	30
5. The Avenger ad on cardboard	$1,000	$1,500	10	10	10	30

* The pulp sendaway offer from "#1" and illustrated Doc Savage Club envelope.

Donald Duck

History: Donald, who emerged long-billed and cranky back in 1934, is about as famous a cartoon image as any non-mouse you can think of.

The Buzz: Ever popular, top ducks bring top bucks, and all of Donald's better pieces are solid 30s on the Quack-O-Meter. We'd all pretty much kill for Barks originals, cels, cartoon posters, early signage, comics (like the complimentary version of "Walt Disney Comics & Stories #4"—a limited subscription lure ca. Christmas 1941), and so on. The only problem is that ducks equal bucks. Buckets of bucks. I don't see significant investible factors in most of these wonderful items, with a few notable exceptions.

Buy it now: *Bisque china toothbrush holders from the 1930s!* These are the only *major* duck goodies that are still well under $1,000 each in mint condition, and they have big four-figure futures. The catch is you have to buy *pristine* mint. No retouches, no repaints. Just the real deal in original condition, with Donald by his lonesome or with his Disney pals. You can't lose if you find these for $500.

Buy it later: Bottlecaps, bread labels (unless they go to a Mickey map), blotters, matchbooks, autographed photos of Daisy Duck.

Watch out: There are many areas with prices so high on the better merch that the appearance of excessive valuation is created. Unless you have been down in the trenches buying and selling duck stuff, don't invest in our friends with the webbed feet. The same rule applies to Donald as to Toonerville Trolleys, Yellow Kid, Al Capp original art and Babe Ruth baseballs (Did Ruth sign all those balls…when did he find time to play?). Specialized markets exists for scores of character collectibles and this is a guide for mainstream investors. It takes time, patience and effort to acquire market savvy on any one special subject. My opinion is that "some markets are self-manipulating." We, the collecting fraternity and active dealers, tend to be seduced by own rarest material. I see that happening a lot lately in what I call "shelf-sitter show-offs." These are things that look good in groups and we all agree are unusually displayable: cookie jars, pitchers, tins, whiskey flasks, lunch boxes, etc. I love to look at a dozen shelves brimming with lunch boxes or thermoses, but If you ask me about collecting Gilligan's Island, Mork & Mindy or Donnie & Marie lunch boxes, which carry prices in the stratosphere, my eyes glaze over. I'm out to lunch, without a box.

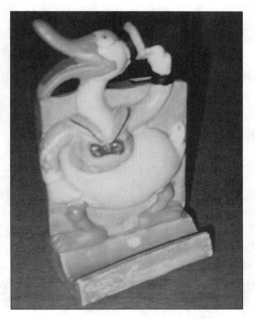

A long-billed toothbrush hold, currently $500, has a projected value of $1,000 for 2004. This holder has a white spot below Donald's feet where the manufacturer missed applying some paint. Don't fix it. Let's leave it the way they made 'em back in the 1930s. The items is still mint (it just has a very minor flaw).

History: Fred Martinek's heroic persona materialized in the comic strips of 1934. Like Spy Smasher, he was a serious patriot. His motto: "Death to Spies," could have been "We Kill for Peace." In fact, his 1930s radio serial evolved into "The Squadron of Peace," and "The League for Defense" during the war.

The Buzz: Boomers never heard of this cat, but as long as there are collectors who remember real radio, some of us will remember Don, Red and the evil world of Scorpia.

Buy it now: Don Winslow periscopes with the store display for $600-$700, and you'll double your money by 2004.

Buy it later: Stuff made from balsa…and Dutch elm or pressed turkey.

Rex Selections: Don Winslow

Item	1999	2004	CF	SF	IF	TF
1. World War II Bubble Gum kit, Fleer.	$900	$1,250	9	9	10	28
2. World War II League for Defense pin	$850	$1,000	9	10	9	28
3. Lt. Commander pin (Martinek's rank).	$800	$950	8	10	10	28
4. Don Winslow periscope and diecut display.	$700	$1,500	9	10	10	29
5. 1939 Squadron of Peace, six-piece kit.	$700	$1,250	9	8	9	26

This 1939 Squadron of Peace six-piece kit, has a present value of $700, with a projected 2004 value of $1,250.

CF-Collectibility Factor; SF-Scarcity Factor; IF-Investibility Factor; TF-Total Factor

How to Become a Member of the Don Winslow Squadron of Peace

This picture shows badge twice actual size

★ To secure membership in the Don Winslow Squadron of Peace and to obtain a regular Squadron of Peace Manual, a copy of the Don Winslow Creed, a Membership Card and a Don Winslow Squadron of Peace Membership Badge, simply address a letter to Don Winslow, Battle Creek, Michigan. Say, "I want to become a member of the Squadron of Peace." *Sign your name and address plainly* and enclose the top from a package of Kellogg's Wheat Krispies and a dime—10 cents—that's all. In a few days you'll receive your complete Squadron of Peace outfit and will become a full-fledged Ensign. Then by fulfilling the requirements shown below you can arrange to be promoted to a Lieutenant-Commander.

This picture shows badge twice actual size

How to Become a Lieutenant-Commander

★ To become a Lieutenant-Commander in the Don Winslow Squadron of Peace you must prove your ability as a Recruiting Officer and a leader. As proof of this

This page from the 1939 Squadron of Peace manual shows the "Ensign" and "Lt. Commander" pins, as well as how to get the Lt. Commander" pin (valued at $800).

History: Two authors, who worked under the names of Danny and Lee (they were cousins), created Ellery Queen in the 1920s. He appeared in every media venue imaginable, and, as I wrote in a magazine article some years back called "Bring Me the Heads of Ellery Queen," he was never fully realized. By that I mean that neither the feature film nor radio/TV action cast in the lead ever quite captured the print character's essence. The Golden Age Ellery Queen was tremendously popular, especially the novels. Radio, plus a dozen films and tele-episodes, prove his staying power. Ralph Bellamy and Hugh Marlowe were okay Ellery Queens, with the tough-voiced William Gargan interesting, and Eddie Quillan the most monumentally miscast.

The Buzz: The Ellery Queen Club Member pinback from radio has become scarce, especially in presentable condition. It's radio gold if you can find it.

Buy it now: "The Case of the Elusive Assassin," an Ellery Queen mystery game. It's a terrific display for this character. Be sure it includes all the figures of Ellery Queen and company.

Buy it later: The Mandarin Mystery posters and any post-war re-release paper.

Rex Selections: Ellery Queen

Item	1999	2004	CF	SF	IF	TF
1. Ellery Queen Club Member pinback	$375	$500	10	10	10	30
2. The Case of the Elusive Assassin Game	$300	$400	10	9	9	28
3. Ellery Queen "Master Detective" title card	$125	$150	10	10	8	28
4. "Close Call for Ellery Queen" title card	$90	$130	8	9	7	24
5. "Desperate Chance for Ellery Queen" title card	$90	$130	8	9	7	24

An impressive item, The Case of the Elusive Assassin game is valued at $300.

23 Elvis

History: I was on the air at a radio station in the early days of 1950s rock, when a package arrived from Sun Records in Tennessee. My memories of a bunch of us sitting around laughing at the name of the new artist "Elvis Presley" are as clear as yesterday. Then we listened to the record and were mesmerized. He had it in the grooves, and no one had it before and no one since. I remained a fan, an on-air fan, and played his records for years, and I was in Dallas when we brought Elvis to the Cotton Bowl. It was like nothing any of us ever witnessed, with the exception of The Beatle's second U.S. tour…The King has left the building.

The Buzz: Yeah, he's still alive. Collectors are the proof, paying $321,500 for his Mercedes limo,

$101,500 for his last Caddy Seville and $101,500 for his stage suit.

Buy it now: Get the authentic old stuff—forget about the booze bottles and modern-day crapola. I mean, if you're going to collect Elvis, *collect Elvis*, ya dig?

Watch out: I've blown every Elvis opportunity I ever had: gave away all the promo presents from Elvis and the Colonel (Parker), threw away all those promo discs and signed Christmas cards, missed the white leather concert belt that went for $17,250 (then proceeded to drop dough at the roulette table), underbid on his own TCOB-in-a-flash jewelry. Geez, Louise, don't listen to me; I'm still trying to find my Hogan's Heroes lunch box!

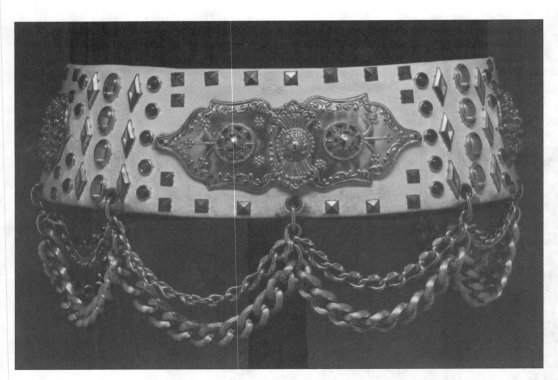

Elvis Presley Concert Stage Belt, early 1970s. (photo courtesy of Butterfield & Butterfield)

History: Michael Arlen created the characters in a 1940 short story called "The Gay Falcon." The Falcon *actually was gay,* that is to say his character's name was "Gay Stanhope Falcon." On radio, he became Michael Waring; Berry Kroeger, James Meighan, Les Damon and Les Tremayne took turns on the mic. There were few characters in which the alter ego name or nickname was left unexplained, but The Falcon was one. Presumably, he'd earned the handle because of his hunting skills or fine eye for detail. When he was counter-programmed against The Shadow, where at 5 p.m. in the Midwest, his sponsor's catchline was, "Avoid 5 O'Clock Shadow! Use Gem Blades.!" By the time he reach

the screen, Gay had become rather soft-boiled, but the movies series held up as durable entertainment in these innocent years. The Falcon made it to TV via syndication.

The Buzz: The Flacon paper is vastly undervalued, and he's beginning to come alive. One-sheets with a $200 future value are still selling from $50-$75. A lot of seven lobbies, titles and 14 x 26-inch inserts were a recent bargain giveaway at only $135.

Buy it now: Yes, do.

The Falcon—A Relative Thing: The two Falcons of World War II B-movies, Tom Conway and George Sanders, were actually brothers in real life.

"The Gay Falcon" color lobby card is a steal at $60.

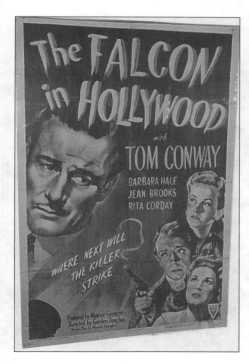

As this guide was being prepared, the author turned down a firm cash offer of $15,000 for the "Superman and the Mole Men: poster and this Flash Gordon "Trip to Mars" 1-sheet from chapter 10 in the serial. This Flash 1-sheet is considered a rare treasure from the Ming (The Merciless) Dynasty!

History: In the 1930s, and only in that decade, America's youth was fascinated with taking fingerprints. There were some fingerprinting techniques used in various anti-crime kits and manuals during World War II, but most of the character kits were issued from 1930-1939.

The Buzz: These toy sets usually don't have high price tags, but there is a modest investment margin, and you can still find sets with unused interior aspects at bargain prices.

Buy it now: Get any sets that were issued in relation to pulp magazines such as *G-Men, Phantom Detective, Nick Carter* and so on. Anything pulp-related has an active market.

Buy it later: Generic G-Men sets, unless the paperwork has a character tie-in like Sherlock Holmes.

Rex Selections: Fingerprint Sets

Item	1999	2004	CF	SF	IF	TF
1. Melvin Purvis	$385	$500	10	9	8	27
2. Nick Carter	$225	$350	10	9.5	7	26.5
3. Dan Fowler (G-Men)	$120	$275	9	9	8	26
4. Gang Busters, 1942, in good condition	$95	$135	8	9	7	24
5. Dick Tracy (small)	$95	$150	9	9	7	25

Melvin Purvis fingerprint set is valued at $385, unused in mailer.

This G-Men fingerprint set with pulp magazine offer has a $120 price tag.

History: Alex Raymond was meticulously drawing a new space character in the latter months of 1933, and Flash Gordon soon premiered. Excluding print pieces, there were less than 50 Golden Age collector's items made, a serious blunder by the marketing people, when one considers the merchandising potential in hindsight. Flash was a wonderfully executed character, with top-notch writing and powerful art: sweeping, lush, visionary work which Raymond manifested with a careful eye to detail. The early radio shows never quite measured up. One of the actors who played the title role—Gale Gordon—assured me in an

As this guide was being prepared, the author turned down a firm cash offer of $15,000 for the "Superman and the Mole Men: poster and this Flash Gordon "Trip to Mars" 1-sheet from chapter 10 in the serial. This Flash 1-sheet is considered a rare treasure from the Ming (The Merciless) Dynasty!

interview that he had a clear memory of premiums that were associated with Flash, but I've never found any. Perhaps in California there were local pieces, but the show was syndicated and that would make premiums highly unlikely. The only other area (other than comics) in which Flash was well promoted was down at the Orpheum, where his trio of chapter plays *killed*. From 1936-1940 and beyond in re-release, "Flash Gordon," "Flash Gordon's Trip to Mars" and "Flash Gordon Conquers the Universe" played to thrilled audiences. Larry "Buster" Crabbe, serial king of the 1930s, and beautiful Jean Rogers, made a perfect screen version of Flash and Dale Arden. What seemed like primitive, deco props and stagy direction now, worked magic when the 1936 chapters flashed across the 50-foot screens of American neighborhood popcorn palaces. We all wanted rockets, ray guns and lead soldiers so we could battle Ming the Merciless at home. Early posters are pure platinum.

Hot Flashes: You probably won't find too many props from the first couple of serials, but they do exist. A canny collectors "stole" the art deco robe worn by Charlie Middleton when he was playing Ming in Universal's first Flash serial for a paltry $15,000! Get the boxed radio repeater version of the clicker pistol, either of the casting sets, mint BLBs from the 1930s, the Golden Age outfit, a Rocket Fighter in near mint with original tailfins and anything from the first serials of 1936.

Buy it now: Get the pair of Dixie Cup portraits. The ones with the blue and lilac backgrounds are going to go way up, so if you can find them original condition for less than $500, snatch them up.

Buy it later: Movie club pins and cards have been overpriced for a long time. I paid a grand for one of the 1936 cards and instantly regretted it. I took a loss of several hundred dollars when I dumped it. Also, I wouldn't be too stoked about shelling out a big price for one of the sets of 1950s Flash Gordon costumes, which were sold in several versions, i.e., with a rinkydink visor and cap, wrist compass, belt with buckle, vest, etc. The box isn't too bad, but I wouldn't go more than $450 for a deluxe set in the box, as a completist. Flash Gordon "Conquers the Universe" posters lack marketplace heat…ditto for pressbooks, cards, serial pins, etc.

Rex Selections: Flash Gordon

Item	1999	2004	CF	SF	IF	TF
1. Flash Gordon's Map of Comics	$2,000	$5,000	10	10	10	30
2. Flash Gordon's Home Foundry, boxed, Ming holding skull aloft	$2,500	$4,000	10	10	10	30
3. Same as item #2, but with different casting	$2,000	$3,500	10	10	10	30
* 4. Flash Gordon Radio Repeater Click Pistol, Marx, boxed	$2,000	$3,500	10	10	10	30
** 5. Flash Gordon Adventure Club 1936 and 1938 pinbacks	$1,200	$2,400	10	10	10	30
6. Flash Gordon's Strange Adventures	$1,000	$1,500	10	10	10	30
*** 7. Flash Gordon's Sparking Ray Gun, boxed	$1,000	$1,500+	10	10	10	30
8. Flash Gordon Siren Pistol, boxed	$900	$1,250	10	10	9.5	29.5
9. Flash Gordon Clicker Pistol, second version	$850	$1,100	10	9.5	9.5	29
10. Flash Gordon Dixiecup Color Portrait, 1936	$550	$1,000	10	8.5	10	28.5
11. Flash Gordon Dixiecup Color Portrait, 1938	$550	$1,000	10	8.4	10	28.4
12. Flash Gordon Club Chicago Herald & Examiner pin	$500	$850	9	9	9.3	27.3
13. Flash Gordon Christmas Lights, 1934, boxed	$700	$900	9	10	8	27
14. Flash Gordon BLBs, four in superior condition	$500	$800	9.5	8	10	27.5
15. Flash Gordon Two-Way Walky-Talker with header	$350	$500	8	9	8	25
16. Flash Gordon and Dale Arden pin set, 1934, pair	$300	$400	9	8	7	24
17. Macy's Battle Fronts Map (Flash and Dale shown)	$200	$250	8	7	7	23
**** 18. Flash Gordon serial 1-sheet	$10,000	$20,000	20	20	20	60
**** 19. Flash Gordon's "Trip to Mars" serial 1-sheet	$7,500	$15,000	20	20	10	50
**** 20. Flash Gordon window card, 1936	$6,000	$10,000	10	20	10	40

* The exquisite toy is unusual because of the box. Marx, not known for its great containers, packaged this one in of the best designed deco boxes I've ever seen.

** The pin where Flash's gun resembles a blunderbuss is from 1940 and is the least valuable, and is generally misidentified.

*** Add the tiny boxed Flash Gordon Sparking Refill, a $75 item, and add $500 to the overall value! It's tough to find but well worth the effort.

**** Items No. 18 to 20 comprise a three-unit wish list—a trio if collectibles will first turn into gold, then into platinum, These are treasures that are from the Mint (the Merciless) Dynasty!

Note the robe that Ming the Merciless is wearing. A smart collector grabbed it for $15,000! A real steal.

Dick Tracy Wrist Radios, boxed with all the goodies: $9,000.

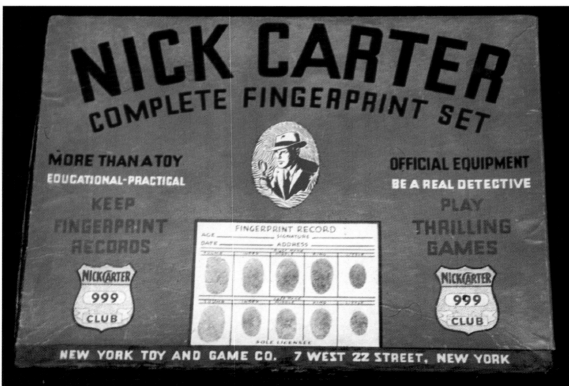

(Top) Various shadow items. (Bottom) Nick Carter Fingerprint Set: $225.

(Top) Pair of Marx Superman Rollover Planes: $12,000. (Bottom) Superman Picture Disc: $300.

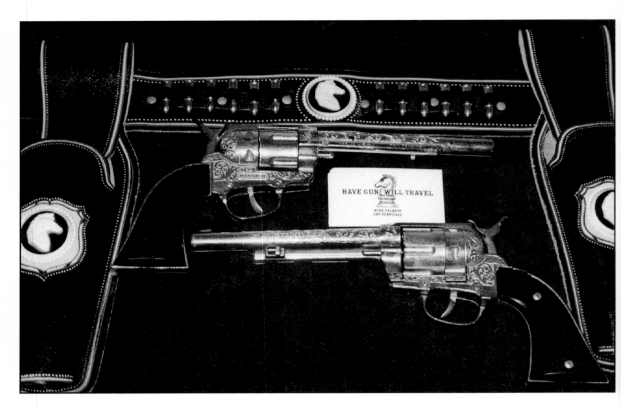

(Top) Pair of Hubley Ricochets from "Have Gun, Will Travel" are $2,500.
(Bottom) The set of four Lone Ranger Frontier Town boxes from 1948 is worth $8,000.

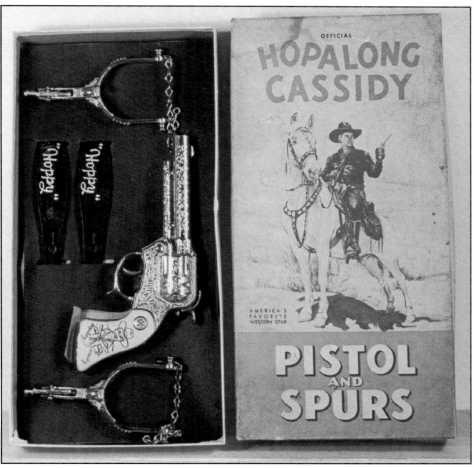

(Top) Hopalong Cassidy Zoomerang Gun, MIB: $300. (Bottom) Hopalong Cassidy Pistols and Spurs from Wyandotte, boxed: $2,100.

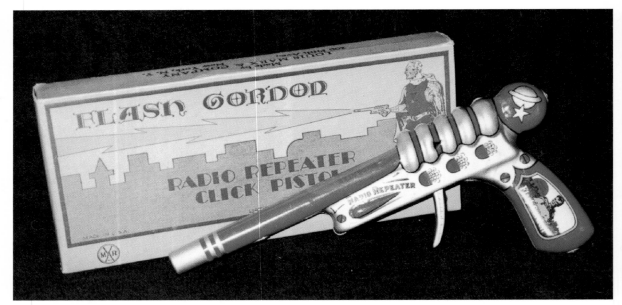

(Top) Flash Gordon Radio Repeater Click Pistol from Marx, boxed: $2,000. (Bottom) Gene Autry Western Pistol, boxed, unfired: $1,500.

(Top) The Seven Dwarfs Shooting Game: $450.
(Bottom) Tarzan in Jungleland, with everything: $5,000+.

The Spider 1931 feature film window card: $700+.

Fu Manchu (and "Yellow Peril")

27

History: "Yellow Peril" was the then-acceptable category name for both a time in America's past and a genre of media product. It was the time of Yellow Hornet Cigars and Yellow Kid comic strips, when a fear or the East became a kind of phobic obsession. Words like "Limehouse" and "Chinatown" were terror-laced buzzwords. Out of this milieu of national yellow fever came writer Sax Rohmer, who breathed life into Dr. Fu, the "Mandarin we loved to hate," in 1913 with the publication of *The Mystery of Dr. Fu-Manchu*. The novel saw first U.S. publication as *The Insidious Dr. Fu Manchu*. His subsequent film, print and broadcast battles were primarily against his nemesis Sir Nayland Smith. Dr. Fu was a kind of super-Moriarty to Sir Nayland's Sherlock, with Dr. Petrie in the Dr. Watson role. It was as if Holmes stories had been turned upside-down and inside-out. I can only think of a few instances in fiction in which the archfiend was more of a leading figure than the protagonist or hero: Milton Caniff's "Dragon Lady vs. Terry" is one obvious example.

(On a personal note, it was Rohmer's work that inspired me to write my series of *Chaingang*© novels, which would become the cornerstone of a dozen books that ultimately sold more than a million copies worldwide. Thanks, Sax.)

Fu Manchu brought total gut-wrenching, delicious terror to audiences back when the earliest crime dramas oozed from out of the glowing Philco tubes, an imaginary dragon clawing its way out of the gothic cathedral radio speakers. It is amazing that the ancestors of today's Standards & Practices (censors) personnel permitted so heavy-duty a horror show back in the 1920s, but they did. "The Collier's Hour" is noteworthy for several heady air treatments of the Rohmer tales that were running in magazine form, as early as the 1920s. Think how listeners must have shivered in genuine fear when Dr. Fu sent his kill-crazy Dacoits on a mission of revenge against Sir Nayland Smith, screaming into the old carbon microphones, "I am the God of Destruction and you will be *destroyed*!", all replete with complex sound effects. A rare 1933 issue of *Radio Guide* contains an illustrated piece that gives tantalizing clues as to the fastidious attention to sounds that went into the radio broadcasts.

"The Mysterious Dr. Fu Manchu" rare color ad, framed, is a $750 best-buy.

This ad from 1930s publicity package includes a menu from a Chinese Restaurant. It has a value of $1,000.

Dr. Fu Manchu was the very essence of what was once called "yellow peril melodrama," and he had many imitators on the air, film and in print. Biograph did a Turn-of-the-Century "Mission of Dr. Foo" silent, for example. Then—in the pulps—came yellow peril clones such as "The Mysterious Wu Fang" and "Dr. Yen Sin" All of this stuff is tremendously collectible today. We're looking for a "fu" good men!

The Buzz: Fu Manchu's cast remains pop culture's most underappreciated characters, and Golden Age memorabilia has a platinum Collectibility, Scarcity and Investibility total that warps the curve. On a scale of 1 to 10, The Devil Doctor is a hard 11.

Buy it now: Everything.

Watch out: Silver Age contemporary movie paper is generally overvalued, as is a one-shot comic.

Rex Selections: Fu Manchu

Item	1999	2004	CF	SF	IF	TF
1. "Drums of Fu Manchu" 3-sheet on linen, 1940 serial advance sheet, 78 x 41 inches, one of the top serials of all time.	$1,500	$3,500	11	11	11	33
2. "Drums of Fu Manchu," Collier's sign	$1,250	$3,000	11	11	11	33
3. "The Shadow of Fu Manchu," 1937 radio package with ad	$1,000	$2,000	10	10	10	30
4. "The Mysterious Dr. Fu Manchu," color ad, framed	$750	$1,000	10	10	10	30
5. "The Return of Dr. Fu Manchu," 1930, set of four jumbo lobbies	$1,500	$2,000	10	10	10	30
6. "Daughter of the Dragon," 1931, window card	$250	$350	10	10	9	29
7. "The Mask of Fu Manchu," promo/giveaway for Karloff film, 1932	$200	$300	10	10	9	29
8. "The Shadow of Fu Manchu"/"Drums of Fu Manchu" pins, each	$150	$200	10	9	9	28
9. "The Shadow of Fu Manchu "keys with envelope and letter	$250	$300	10	10	8	28
10. *Hand of Fu Manchu* and *Return of Dr. Fu Manchu* hardcover reprints, with dust jackets, Grosset & Dunlap, pair	$150	$200	10	10	8	28

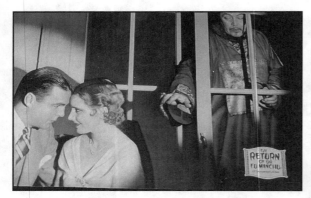

One of four jumbo lobby cards from "The Return of Dr. Fu Manchu," 1930, ultra-rare. The set of four is valued at $1,500.

Another of the four jumbo lobby cards from "The Return of Dr. Fu Manchu."

28

Gang Busters

History: Writer-producer Phillips H. Lord, who became famous in the radio era for such successes as Seth Parker, brought Gang Busters to the air in 1936. The introductory signature, a pound sound montage of marching feet and machine-gun fire, gave us the expression, "it comes on like Gang Busters," a phrase still part of America's working vocabulary more than 60 years later.

The Buzz: No collector of radio or TV premiums feels his showcase is complete without a couple of items from Gang Busters. It's one of the first vintage shows one associates with exciting radio, up there with The Shadow, The Green Hornet and I Love a Mystery. Modestly priced Gang Busters stuff still affords today's collector a decent opportunity in the marketplace.

Buy it now: Get the Marx Sub-Machine Gun if you can find one with the wooden stock firmly attached to the metal part. It's a design flaw that usually results well-used toys being in fragile shape.

Gang Busters Shield, Style B, ca. 1942, $75.

Buy it later: The high-priced serial memorabilia is probably not going anywhere.

Watch out: I'd stay away from blotters, matchbooks or Gang Busters Bug Zappers made from two blocks of wood (place bug on Block A and hit with Block B).

Gang Busters Finger Print Kit. This one, in about good condition, sold for $95.

Rex Selections: Gang Busters

Item	1999	2004	CF	SF	IF	TF
* 1. Gang Busters Crusade Against Crime Sub-Machine Gun, sparking	$800	$1,000+	10	10	10	30
2. Gang Busters Keywind Squad Car, complete and working....	$700	$1,000	10	10	10	30
3. Gang Busters Crusade Against Crime Tie, on store display header	$375	$500	10	10	9	29

Item	1999	2004	CF	SF	IF	TF
4. Gang Busters belt and buckle with original paint	$275	$400	10	10	9	29
5. Gang Busters wallet with rare membership card............	$200	$300	10	10	9	29
6. Gang Busters Game in premium mailer from radio show.....	$175	$300	10	10	8	28
7. "Gang Busters" serial 1-sheet	$150	$200	9	9	8	26
** 8. Gang Busters comic book with shield on back cover......	$175	$250	9	9	8	26
9. Gang Busters Tin Target Set, generic gun and darts	$145	$200	9	9	8	26
10. Gang Busters Game, 1941............................	$85	$110	8	9	8	25
11. Gang Busters Finger Print Kit	$95+	$150	8	9	8.5	25.5
*** 12. Gang Busters BLBs, all the small-format books, each...	$100	$225	9	10	9	28
13. Gang Busters Shield, Style A, 1930s, star border	$75	$125	9	8	9	26
14. Gang Busters cap, a bargain	$65	$150	8	9	9	26
15. Gang Busters Shield, tin, Style C	$75	$125	9	9	9	27

* This value is only for the guns with the wood stock attached firmly to the colorful tin toy's receiver.

** To my knowledge, the only Golden Age comics with premiums on the backs were Gang Busters books. This one shows shield style B, ca. 1942.

*** Many of these books are worth picking up in the $75-$125 range, as they will likely have values of $150-$300 by 2003

Left: Gang Busters Wallet with rare Membership Card, $200; right: tie with display, $375.

> **CF-Collectibility Factor; SF-Scarcity Factor;**
> **IF-Investibility Factor; TF-Total Factor**

History: Autry's songs, Western movies, radio and television programs, countless in-person appearances, successes in virtually every area of media and entertainment, not to mention investments in everything from oil fields to The Field of Dreams adds up to…legend!

The Buzz: We all want the same stuff with Gene's name: cap guns and holsters, boxed treasures, signage—in particular from this milestone 1935 chapter play, "The Phantom Empire."

Buy it now: Deluxe gun sets, especially with spurs, mintish condition Whitman's, Dell comics, strips (1940 was a hot year), and anything from the Melody Ranch, both the radio show and the place (Phantom Empire's feature edit was released as "Radio Ranch"). Pillsbury radio premiums start at around $200 in original shape, and they aren't that easy to find. Even radio mags with Autry covers are collectible.

Buy it later: Loose horseshoe nails.

Pasadena: Cardboard guns, matchbooks—anything where the ink smells fresh.

This tin-can robot head prop from "The Phantom Empire" sold for almost $7,500 a few years back.

This lot of three mint cap guns is currently valued at $650, with an expected retail price of $1,000.

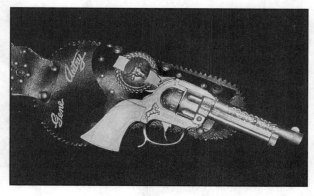

Gene Autry Gun in holsters is a $400 item, with a probable value of $850 by 2004.

Rex Selections: Gene Autry

Item	1999	2004	CF	SF	IF	TF
* 1. Prop from "The Phantom Empire," tin-can robot head	$7,475	$10,000+	10	10	10	30
2. Western Pistol in box, unfired	$1,500	$2,000	10	10	10	30
3. Double six-gun set with holsters in box.	$1,400	$3,000	10	10	10	30
4. Double six-gun set with fringed holsters/matching spurs, no box	$850	$1,200	10	10	10	30
5. Gun in holsters, no box	$400	$850	10	10	10	30
6. Ranch Outfit in box, good	$450	$900	10	10	10	30
** 7. Lot of three mint cap guns	$650	$1,000	10	8.5	10	28.5
8. Gene Autry "In Person" pop-up sign, 1930s	$250	$350	10	9	9	28
9. Gene Autry #100, mint file copy	$100	$150	8	10	8	28
10. Souvenir Program (Autry with Annie Oakley) and unused ticket	$95	$150	9	8	9	26

* A two-step provenance is a must.

** Includes small Buzz Henry, cast iron with red signature on white grips, small with red plastic stone and orange-red grips.

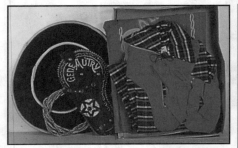

The actual outfit from the Gene Autry Ranch Outfit; complete and in the box, this sells for $450.

The outside of the box to the Gene Autry Ranch Outfit.

Gene Autry #100, mint file copy, is worth about $100 now.

This Souvenir Program with Gene Autry and Annie Oakley and unused ticket is a good purchase at $95.

This Gene Autry "In Person" pop-up sign from the 1930s has a retail price of $250.

History: These four characters of screen and print fame are unrelated beyond their colorful names. All of their memorabilia could be termed as scarce and sought-after, excluding modern-day stuff like the Mego Green Lantern action figures and contemporary Green Lantern rings…well, that's not exactly true, either. All their memorabilia is sought, now that I think about it.

The Buzz: You gotta bring some green to get some green.

Rex Selections: Green Archer/Arrow/Lama/Lantern

Item	1999	2004	CF	SF	IF	TF
* 1. Green Archer Pressbook from sound serial, uncut	$175	$350	10	10	10	30
** 2. Green Lama Escapo Victory Fold-Out	$300	$600	10	10	10	30
3. Green Lantern costume, unused in box with mask	$175	$325	10	10	10	30

* The 1940 version of the earlier silent-era chapters can be collected in this one unit, which shows all the posters, interesting premiums and exploitation devices like arrows, feathers and membership cards in the Green Archer Club.

** The World War II comic book "trick" fold-out. Two versions exist and both are scarce.

Green Lama Escapo
Victory Fold-Out
has a $300 value.

Serial card from Green Archer Pressbook. The pressbook, mint and uncut, is worth $175 today.

History: Devised by Detroit-area broadcaster George W. Trendle in the mid-1930s, The Green Hornet was co-created by Trendle and Fran Striker in the mold of The Lone Ranger, who'd been a major rider on the radio range for three years. The Green Hornet overflowed the coffers of The Michigan Network with sponsor money. Britt Reid was a relative of the masked Texas Ranger, and the parallels (Tonto/Kato, Silver/Black Beauty, etc.) are fun to look for. The Green Hornet was a smash in every medium, just as The Lone Ranger had been before him.

The Buzz: The Green Hornet's buzz sounds like this—ka-ching! That's sounds remarkably like a cash register.

Buy it now: Absolutely almost all of it! Any super-nice Green Hornet BLBs from the Golden Age are a bargain for less than $100.

Watch out: Unless you're bent on cornering the market in Hornet TV-era goodies, I'd be a tad cautious getting into serious bidding wars for things like the "Bike Badge" Sendaway's molded sign from the 1960s. The last one that sold went for three-huge, and that's a handful of green to lay out for something most of us aren't Jonesin' for. Can you dig? I knew you could.

Reproduced pin: The 1939 Universal Adventure Club serial pin was reproduced. Being able to pick the original from the reproduction is important as the original is a $1,000 item and the reproduction sells for $1. Here's the way to tell the difference between the original and reproduction:

Original pin: light pale blue wings; the body was orange with yellow and green stripes on the hornet's body; the background was dark green.

Stay away with anything with the word "bag" in it, like the trick or treat bag.

Reproduction pin: vivid blue wings; the body is orange with green stripes, but no yellow on stripes, the only yellow is on the upper and lower sections of the hornet; the background is medium green.

Take a pass completely: Anything with the word "bag" in it, like trick or treat "bag," vendor "bag," vomit "bag," "bag" lady, etc.

Rex Selections: The Green Hornet

Item	1999	2004	CF	SF	IF	TF
1. Advance color 1-sheet poster, 1939 (see color section)	$4,500	$6,000	10	10	10	30
2. Official Green Hornet Reporter's Kit, 1938	$1,500	$3,500	10	10	10	30
3. The Green Hornet Secret Seal Ring with papers, boxed, 1947	$3,750	$6,000	10	10	10	30
4. Green Hornet comic with original cover art for "green skulls".	$2,500	$3,500	10	10	10	30
5. Lobby card showing Britt and Kato.	$400	$750	10	9	10	29
6. Glass from GJM set, "Green Hornet," 1930s	$300	$600	10	9	10	29

Item	1999	2004	CF	SF	IF	TF
* 7. Green Hornet Halloween costume and mask, unused in box	$1,465	??	10	10	9?	29?
8. Corgi Green Hornet Black Beauty with figures and accessories in unusual pop-out display box (see color section)	$1,500	$5,500	10	9	10	29
9. Aurora Green Hornet Black Beauty model kit	$1,500	$5,500	10	10	9	29
** 10. Green Hornet Lucky Coin and letter.	??	??	10	10	10	30

* This item old together with a Captain Action costume for $1,465.

** I don't know of any collectors who've turned up with mid-1930s piece, but I was told it was George W. Trendle's first Green Hornet hardware item. The value would be ultra-high.

This lobby ard showing Britt and Kato is a $400 item.

Mintish Green Hornet BLBs are a bargain for less than $100.

Green Hornet comic with original cover art for "green skulls" (art not shown, just the comic book). Together, the comic and art are valued at $2,500.

This Green Hornet glass from 1930s GJM set is valued at $300, with a chance of doubling in value by 2004.

Corgi Green Hornet Black Beauty with figures and accessories in unusual pop-out display box, a bargain today for $1,500.68-24.

History: Actor William Boyd had three careers in Hollywood, spanning silents and early talkies (in which he was the leading man in melodramas); as a Western star from the 1930s through the late-1940s; and again when Hopalong shows rode out of the radios and early TV sets, selling bread, milk and cereal. His image was everywhere. Today, Hopalong remains one of the most identifiable images and his popularity resists definition. His movie magic was as mesmerizing and unexplainable as Edgar Bergen's on radio. Even in the 1950s, the silver-haired star drew kids to his in-person appearances like a magnet, and I was one of them. I'm a Hoppy collector to this day. When they tore down the old Jo Theater where we went to see Boyd and Topper and got fake "silver" dollars with Hopalong's image, I saved the marquee 2-sheet frame (a Lash Larue sheet from 1947, framed and frozen in time, adorns my patio). Hopalong's pictures were hardly action-filled by the time we began watching his TV shows; they were slow-moving and talky by comparison, but we *loved* them. I guess you had to be there.

The Buzz: I'd hate to be a Hopalong completist. I was once privileged to own a collection of things a grateful Boyd had once given to the son of his cosmetic surgeon after a particularly successful nip-and-tuck. It was a *wardrobe carton* packed wall-to-wall with boxed guns, steer's head neckerchief slides and even a bedspread! Every conceivable product once carried his world-famous image: the good guy in the black hat.

When you're talking about Hoppy, you can find every piece of promotional purveyance from pillar to post, and any product tie-in from Pillsbury to Post. *You da man, Hoppy!* One version of the Aladdin Hoppy lunch box and thermos is reportedly valued at $5,000! Now there's a chow set! Oddly enough, I've never found any original Hopalong Cassidy posters from the 1930s; posters have been widely reproduced.

Buy it now: Mint, unfired guns, boxed, if possible. However, C-10 condition cap pistols (with or without holster, box or cartridges) are only rising in value. Store displays, cereal boxes...all the rare stuff is vanishing!

Buy it later: Pinbacks, pictures, non-Western stuff like popcorn boxes and hair trainer bottles, in-

This Hopalong Cassidy Wyandotte scrimshaw-style pistol/spurs, boxed is a beauty that sells for $2,100 today, and likely more than $3,000 in the future.

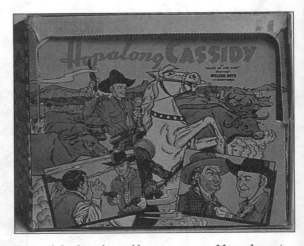

Part of the lot of two film viewers and boxed movie sets that is valued at $575.

stitutional prize-type stuff and Savings Club materials are a bit off the mark. Unless it has great displayability—like lunch boxes, saddlebags, Western wear, guns, hats, bandannas—concentrate on other areas. Hoppy comics, naturally, are a smokin' field unto themselves.

Watch out: A bunch of smalls have been reproduced. The good news is that most of the pins are pretty easy to differentiate from the originals. Hoppy holsters have been reproduced—and beautifully.

Hoppy under $100. This "Bill Boyd" Dixiecup portrait carries a $95 price.

Hoppy under $100. This World War II Herald from Pressbook is a good buy at $45.

Hoppy under $100. This Deluxe Coloring book is valued at $90.

Rex Selections: Hopalong Cassidy

Item	1999	2004	CF	SF	IF	TF
* 1. Deluxe, boxed Hoppy double-gun and holster set	$2,750	$3,850	10	10	10	30
2. Hopalong Cassidy cereal box, badges and store display	$2,360	$3,500	10	10	10	30
3. Hopalong Cassidy store sign with prototype premium artwork	$2,200	$3,000	10	10	10	30
4. Hopalong Cassidy Wyandotte scrimshaw-style pistol/spurs, boxed	$2,100	$3,000+	10	10	10	30
5. Hopalong Cassidy gold-plated single-shot pistol with signature on black grips, unfired, mint in box	$1,500	$2,750	10	10	10	30
6. Cap pistol, shadow-boxed, scrimshaw-style, unfired, mint. . . .	$975	$1,400	10	10	10	30
** 7. Four versions of Hoppy's steer's head bandanna slides, all .	$580	$900	10	10	10	30
8. Hoppy Nite-Light and Bunkhouse Lamp set, for both	$555	$1,000	10	10	10	30
*** 9. Hopalong Cassidy Zoomerang Gun, mint in box	$300	$450	10	10	10	30
10. Lot of two film viewers and boxed movie sets	$575	$700	10	10	10	30

* This set has "scrimshaw" type grips depicting Hopalong, black belt and holsters with silver and gold honchos. It is gorgeous and highly prized. It sold for $2 back in 1950.

** This lot of four includes the Branding Iron premium with instructions. This device was a well-designed plastic head that stamped "HC" onto paper, and was one of the most interesting items in the giveaway wardrobe carton mentioned earlier.

*** This is typical of the lesser Hoppy pieces that are now picking up rapidly in value.

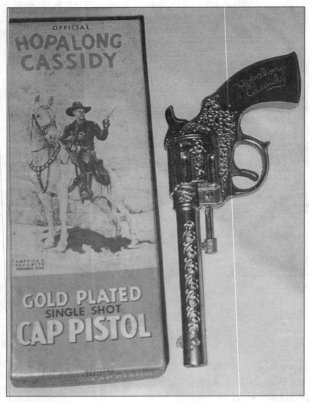

The Hoppy Nite-Light (shown here) and Bunkhouse Lamp set can fetch more than $550.

Hopalong Cassidy gold-plated single-shot pistol with signature on black grips, unfired, mint in box, will set you back $1,500.

This Hopalong Cassidy Zoomerang Gun, mint in box, sells for $300 today.

William Boyd is wearing one of his famous steer's head bandanna slides, which came in many versions.

History: Hop hit the comics around 1939, the radio air soon after. He was considered strictly a wartime character by most of us, and the radio serial had lost its currency by the time the chapter play came out in the post-war 1940s. Hop belongs to that era when we were still fascinated by prop- and piston-planes, and heroes could seriously be named Speed, Hop, Tank, Buzz and (my fave) Downwind.

The Buzz: Hop is just starting to happen. Premiums, mint and complete in the mailers, have a specific, undeniable charm to us old kids who liked planes n' stuff.

Buy it now: Premiums, store displays, cereal boxes, All-American Comics.

Buy it later: Chapter play paper. At the Bijou, Hop was a flop.

Watch out: Don't overpay for the photographs. There are a couple of portrait giveaways, one photograph and one art with imprint signature.

Frankenstein," framed and matted 1932 ad for London film release, is a $550+ item.

Rex Selections: Hop Harrigan

Item	1999	2004	CF	SF	IF	TF
* 1. Lot of Hop Harrigan items	$2,000	$4,000	10	11	10	31
2. Hop Harrigan Atomic Bomb Adventure Kit, in mailer box, with complete set of Cocoa Marsh films	$300	$500	9	10	10	29
3. Atomic All-American Flying Club Wings and comic book offer	$300	$450	9.5	9	9	27.5
4. WWII Flying club, 5-part kit with cloth insignia replacing badge	$100	$175	9	9	8	26
5. All-American Observation Corps cloth insignia	$100	$175	9	9	8	26

* The best I've seen, bid on or owned is the following lot of 1945 radio premiums from the Gold Collection, which were sold by Christie's as a single unit: 1) 9-1/2 x 13-1/2-inch illustrated mailer, three marble bombs in envelope and a 1945 Target Map for the Superfortress; 2) Hop's Boeing B-29 Superfortress Model Plane, Built-In Secret Bombsight, two mirrors; 3) all seven units of the Para-Plane radio offer, each about 15 x 5-1/2 inches, including Fuselage, Parachutists, Parachute, illustrated mailer, Damaged Plane, Secret Code Signal Blinker, Flying Helicopter Model and game accessories (including launching tube); 4) 18 x 13-inch rectangular store sign; 5) 20 x 16-inch horizontal box and premium diecut display; 6) 16 x 15-inch diecut vertical display, uniquely rare, from the men who created the premiums, Sam and Gordon Gold.

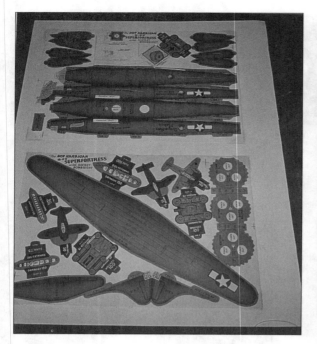

Hop's Boeing B-29 Superfortress Model Plane, Built-In Secret Bombsight, two mirrors, from Gold Collection.

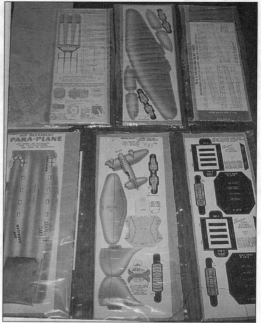

All seven units of the Para-Plane radio offer, each about 15 x 5-1/2 inches, including Fuselage, Parachutists, Parachute, illustrated mailer, Damaged Plane, Secret Code Signal Blinker, Flying Helicopter Model and game accessories (including launching tube), from Gold Collection.

Hop Harrigan 18 x 13-inch rectangular store sign, from Gold Collection.

History: The Golden Age touchstones of horror scared audiences half to death in the early-1930s, with Mary Shelley's "Frankenstein" and the heir of Bram Stoker's Nosferatu, "Dracula," breaking all box-office records. Between Fu Manchu on radio and Frankenstein's monster, plus Dracula in the movies, kids were sleeping with the lights on during most of 1931 and 1932.

The Buzz: This is memorabilia that leads the pack in terms of pricey print and film collectibles. Unless you have between $90,000 and $250,000 to indulge your collecting whims, you'll need to collect smart.

Buy it now: Look for the off-beat and unusual in movie paper from the primary characters (Frankenstein, Dracula, The Mummy, The Wolfman), but, above all, The Creature. "The Creature from the Black Lagoon" and sequels are probably the hottest current horror titles. Best buys: black-and-white or black-and-white with color frameable ads, heralds, press kit handbills, promo sheets (especially the double-page poster-type), showman's manuals, exhibitor displays. The more unusual, the better. Golden Age crossovers ("Dracula's Daughter," "Frankenstein Meets The Wolfman," "Mark of the Vampire" and "Abbott & Costello Meet Frankenstein") are bargain titles, even when seemingly going for inflated numbers. Scarcer model kits, too.

Buy it later: Modern-day Frankendreck, Mummy Sequels, Abbott & Costello Meet...The Killer, Invisible Man, etc.

Frankenstein," framed and matted 1932 ad for London film release, is a $550+ item.

Watch out: Don't overpay for good-looking peripheral stuff, such as Inner Sanctum titles ("Frozen Ghost" and "Calling Mr. Death"). Ditto for cult pieces such as "Devil Bat's Daughter."

On Fire: Ignore conventional wisdom on movie paper that says not to buy re-release material Real-art re-release paper is absolutely *on fire*!

Rex Selections: Horror

Item	1999	2004	CF	SF	IF	TF
1. Original "Dracula" window card, green and orange version	$7,000	$10,000	10	10	10	30
2. "The Creature Walks Among Us" 1-sheet on linen	$1,500	$2,500	10	10	10	30

What follows are some super-scarce pieces, priced at less than $600 each, that have a scary-good future. High Collectibility, maximum Scarcity and unbeatable Investibilty guarantee these "take it to the bank" horror collectibles.

Item	1999	2004	CF	SF	IF	TF
3. "Frankenstein," framed and matted 1932 ad for London film release, image area is 12-3/4 x 9-1/4 inches	$565	$800+	10	11	10	31
4. "Horror Island," title card, color, 1941, old B-Western stars in a horror/old dark house title, gorgeous	$355	$600	10	9	10	29

Item	1999	2004	CF	SF	IF	TF
5. "Creature from the Black Lagoon," framed 18 x 12-inch showman's manual for both 3-D and 2-D release exploitation, 1954	$380	$650	10	10	10	30
6. "Abbott & Costello Meet Frankenstein," green, black and white, 18-1/2 x 12-inch trade promo, 1940s, would be great framed	$295	$400	10	10	9	29
7. "Bride of Frankenstein," 18-inch purple theater tease, 1935. . .	$250	$400	10	10	9	29
8. "Dracula's Daughter," 18 x 12-1/4-inch two-page promo, 1939, ultra bargain	$190	$350	9	10	10	29
9. *Horror Stories* pulp, "Dracula's Brides"	$95	$150	9	9	9.5	27.5
10. "Mark of the Vampire," Lugosi handbill	$75	$150	9	9	9.5	27.5

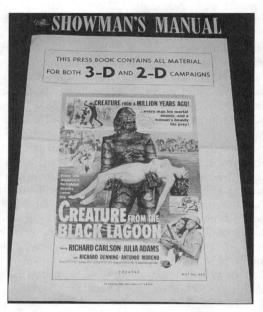

"Creature from the Black Lagoon," framed 18 x 12-inch showman's manual for both 3-D and 2-D release exploitation, has a current price of $380.

A 9-1/2 x 13-1/2-inch illustrated mailer, three marble bombs in envelope and a 1945 Target Map for the Superfortress, from Gold Collection.

This "Dracula's Daughter," 18 x 12-1/4-inch two-page promo, is an ultra bargain under $200.

"Abbott & Costello Meet Frankenstein," green, black and white, 18-1/2 x 12-inch trade promo from the 1940s is a good find at less than $300.

Horror Stories pulp, "Dracula's Brides" is a $95 item.

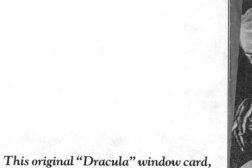

"Horror Island," title card, color, starred old B-Western stars; it has a $355 price tag.

This original "Dracula" window card, green and orange version, is a $7,000 item that could top $10,000 by 2004.

35

Howdy Doody

History: His experimental appearance in 1947 changed the future: adults who would one day raise The Latch-Key Generation, with the aid of the "World's Greatest Babysitter." TV might have realized its ambitious goal, to truly become a window on the world, but, like commercial radio, it became a venue for American commerce—a money machine. By 1948, Howdy Doody had a home for life. Howdy was a product-moving powerhouse, delivering incredible results to clients. He was almost single-handedly responsible for radio's demise, years before Top 40, as big accounts moved to the new medium in droves when ad people saw how the shelves cleared of Ovaltine.

The Buzz: You love him or you hate him. Collectors fight tooth-and-nail for top merch. A Howdy "room," replete with bed, television, chair, floor and table lamps, wallpaper, drapes, ceiling lamp, table—the whole Howdy enchilada—is currently valued at $10,000-$15,000, with a potential of $25,000 or more by 2003. Big display pieces, complete and mint, cost top dollar and buying is super-competitive.

Buy it now: Collectibles in the $200-$400 range offer a good Investibility margin. Get your Howdy Doody premiums in the mailers, or—if you're loaded—go after the great toys like the wind-up band

Howdy Doody Jigsaw.

and the more difficult-to-find boxed collectibles. You don't have to spend a kazillion bucks to get great looking displayables. Just because you don't want to shell out $1,500 for a mint Howdy Doody cereal box with cut-outs, all is not lost: get some Royal Pudding boxes with cut-outs, save $1,300 and take someone you love to the riverboat.

Clarabell has spoken.

Howdy Doody Christmas Cards.

Howdy Doody Air-O-Doodle on card.

Rex Selections: Howdy Doody

Howdy you do? The five selections listed below all have Total Factors of 29 and are selling for less than $300 each:

    1. Howdy Doody Animated Puppet, unpunched, Three Musketeers
    2. Howdy Doody Quiz Show, Kagran Corp.
    3. Howdy Doody Jigsaw, Poll Parrot
    4. Howdy Doody Air-O-Doodle on card, Kargran
    5. Howdy Doody Christmas Cards, Mars, Inc.

Howdy Doody Quiz Show.

Howdy Doody Animated Puppet, unpunched, Three Musketeers.

91

36

Jack Armstrong

History: Jack Armstrong, The All-American Boy, picked up for Wheaties and General Mills where Skippy left off, bringing strong adventure-theme serial to radio in 1933. Jack, Tom Mix and the Lone Ranger roared, fired and thundered across the kilocycles about the same time and became, coincidentally, the cornerstones of juvenile radio. The post-war Jack Armstrong show suffered mightily in writing and agency promotions. Gone were the days of Mystical Dragon Talismans and Secret (Nordic-like) Bomb-Site offers woven into the bread of the plots. The 1930s-1944 Jack Armstrong was the real cereal serial deal. How do you explain Jack? (Someone just asked me, "Who *was* Jack Armstrong?") That's a tough question. He was a kid aviator with a father-figure named Uncle Jim Fairfield and two cousins named Billy and Betty. Beyond that, what can I tell you?

The Buzz: Armstrongiana is the province of older collectors, by and large, and the young premium fans are just beginning to get hip to this mother of all sendaway shows.

Buy it now: Focus on the great stuff…three Jack Armstrong cereal-box items were on the shelves in 1933 alone, and usually they can still be found for less than $500 each. The Secret Whistle Code rings and paper code—which have been reproduced and faked—are still way underpriced. The set of Jack Armstrong Adventure boxes, the Magic Answer Box, the Sky Ranger Plane giveaway, the Sound Effects Kit, the Bomb-Site, store signs, the Chart Game, Schoenke original art from the strips and

Two of the seven items described in #3.

books are some of the things to look for now. Pedometers are still cool.

Buy it later: BLBs, comics, Explorer Scopes, stamp sets, flashlights, sports stuff (Big Ten Football Game), photos without a mailer, Tru-Flite fighters without a mailer (these were reproduced, first by GMI, then others from 1944 through the 1960s). After the late-1940s, Jack's show was nothing but a lot of "Jeepers-creepers, Uncle Jack!" type of dialogue so the kids could follow the story. The later memorabilia from Armstrong of the SBI is irrelevant.

Rex Selections: Jack Armstrong

Item	1999	2004	CF	SF	IF	TF
* 1. 1933 Wheaties boxes	$500+	$1,500+	10	10	10	30
* 2. 1933 Wheaties box with Shooting Planes offer with the planes (discs) and silver gun in box, for all	$750+	$2,000+	10	10	10	30
** 3. 1936 Chart game—Adventures with the Mystical Dragon Talismans, mint and uncut playing pieces and spinner, color labels from "Dragon" and "Talisman" citrus products, museum shadow-boxed with a portrait light, rare	$3,500	$5,000	10	11	10	31
4. Listening Squad hardware, 1940-1941, any piece, rare	$1,000+	$3,000+	10	10	10	30
5. Sky Ranger Plane, 1940 Wheaties box	$600	$850	10	10	9	29
6. Jack Armstrong Wrist Compass in mailer, 1938	$600	$850	10	10	9	29

* These boxes range from Jack's Training Secrets to sports equipment, but the box I want is the one with the Shooting Planes offer, as shown in the 1933 comic strips. Now that's sorting the Wheaties from the chaff! Consider, for frame of reference, that a 1933 Coca-Cola bottle-shaped radio has brought a bid of almost $4,600 at auction.

** This is one of the most beautiful and dramatic radio premiums ever made.

A montage of Jack Armstrong items. "Wave the flag for Hudson High, boys…"

37 *The Lone Ranger*

History: Few Golden Age characters have been as powerful or enduring as the masked Texas Ranger conceived for radio by George W. Trendle and Fran Striker. He was the best radio could offer in the early-1930s, a careful amalgam of sound effects and sh-tick that would fire his legend deep into our collective sub-conscious. We *believed*, back then, in what The Lone Ranger stood for, that he an Tonto were on our side, and, when the great silver horse reared up on his hind legs and whinnied, we *saw* him, with the most amazing camera ever invented—the mind's eye.

The Buzz: He had the best premiums, signs, maps...you name it. Companies such as Silvercup Bread (a perfect "Silver" tie-in) and General Mills (kids thought General Mills was a man in World War II) sponsored The Lone Ranger for two decades. Catch-phrases like "Heigh-Yo Silver" became military passwords and are as much a part of the American vocabulary now as they were 60 years ago. Unlike other fictional heroes, many of the actors who played The Lone Ranger seemed to have been born to play the part: Brace Beemer on radio; Lee Powell and Bob Livingston in the 1930s chapters; and Clay Moore on TV helped breathe life into the legend. Not only is great fun to collect this stuff, but as investibles go, it's like having your own silver mine. Everything from Charles Flanders' original art to ad agency file materials catches fire when it hits the collectibles marketplace. Lone Ranger collectors are often completists. Thus a set of Lone Ranger and Tonto arcade cards is disproportionately

1938 serial ad, "after 4 years of waiting," red, black and white. It's a wish-list item valued at what the market will bear.

more valuable than a group of 15 scarce cards. The same applies to Frontier Towns and other such items.

Marx Click Pistol with decal in box, unused and mint, is a $750+ item.

Buy it now: The repros, fakes and fantasies are pretty easy to identify (so far), and if you do your homework and don't get nuts, you'll be okay, Kemo Sabe. Go for all of it. Keywind toys, boxed movie viewers, Western ranch outfits, scrapbooks—it's all neat stuff.

Rare Lone Ranger pin and decoder with unbent tab.

This Lone Ranger Merita Bread Drawing in frame is usually priced at $200 or more.

Rex Selections: The Lone Ranger

Item	1999	2004	CF	SF	IF	TF
* 1. Premium and store gun prototypes with papers/other accessories. . . . .$2,000+		$5,000+	13	13	14	40
** 2. Lone Ranger Frontier Town, uncut and mint $9,000		$12,000	10	10	10	30
*** 3. Lone Ranger Meteorite Ring $16,000		$25,000	10	10	10	30
4. Lone Ranger Ice Cream Cone Comic #1, 1939-1940 . . . .$4,000		$6,000	10	10	10	30
5. Lone Ranger color standees, any version . . . .$1,000+		$3,000	10	10	10	30
6. Lone Ranger Kix Airbase with one cereal box $500		$750	10	10	10	30
7. Lone Ranger Silvercup Hunt Map with illustrated mailer. $400		$600	10	9	10	29
8. Lone Ranger Merita Bread Drawing in frame . . . . $200+		$400	10	9	10	29

The following items can sometimes be found in the $50+ range, but more often in the hundreds:

9. Lone Ranger Horseshoe Badge (many versions)
10. Lone Ranger six-pointed stars (many versions)
11. Lone Ranger Merita kit with badge, bullet, letter, picture
12. Lone Ranger glow-in-the-dark Saddle Ring with film
13. Lone Ranger Flashlight Pistol with lenses for code signals
14. Lone Ranger Silver bullet pencil sharpener
15. Lone Ranger Kix Atomic Bomb Ring

Here are some "wish list" pieces, without prices, meaning the value is what the market will bear:

16. 1938 serial ad, "after 4 years of waiting," red, black and white
17. Complete set of Whitman BLBs in mint

18. Complete set of Grosset & Dunlap hardcovers with dust jackets in mint
19. Gun set in holsters
20. Complete set of secret compartment rings with inserts
21. Complete set of all 10 silver bullets

* These are at the top of this section. Any prototype model of a Lone Ranger gun with artwork, paper items, cereal or product container (a full display, in other words), will bring at least $2,000-$4,000 now, with a $5,000-$10,000 estimate five years from now. The sky's the limit. Some of the items tied to this wonderfully marketed hero include WXYZ's Wild West Pop Gun from 1933, Silvercup's Target Set, Morton's Salt Repeating Gun and Targets, Republic Serial Exhibitor Advertising Pop-Gun, Marx Click Pistol with decal, Kilgore Repeating Cap Pistol with variations of hammer, grips, etc., 1946 Marx Target Game with gun and darts (prototype would be worth $5,000 or more already), Flashlight Pistol, Six-Gun Ring, TV Rubber Band Gun, Marx Smoking Clicker Gun.

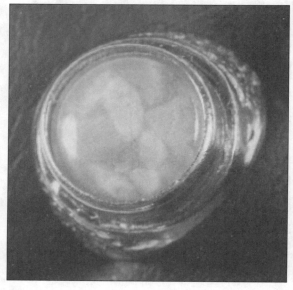

Priced at $16,000, this is only one of two authenticated Lone Ranger Meteorite Rings.

** This 1948 Cheerios premium sendaway and package-back liquidator consists of four ground plans and four punch-out sections in mailers. There are also nine box backs, which, still on boxes and uncut with all parts in mint condition, has a $9,000 value. A Frontier Town with all four ground plans and four punch-out sections and nine box backs cut, but with the pieces intact on the Cheerios backs is $4,000 ($6,000 in 2003). A Frontier Town single section with ground plans and one complete box in mint is $1,100 ($2,200 in 2003). Boxes themselves start at about $450.

*** One of two authenticated. The other is in General Mills' permanent archives. This was a Lone Ranger test in 1942 and only 85 were shipped. This ring was reissued with two different contents as the Gold Ore Ring, by another company—the exterior appears to be the same, but it isn't a Meteorite Ring. (See metallurgist's examination in *Premiums Magazine*.)

Display store sign for Morton's Salt Repeating Gun and Targets. This is a prototypical piece form the Christie's auction of Sam and Gordon Gold items. (photo courtesy of Christie's East)

The comic strip offer for The Lone Ranger Frontier Town. The strip is valued at $25.

Lone Ranger Flashlight Pistol with lenses for code signals.

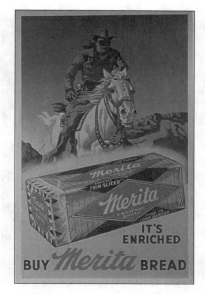

This Lone Ranger Merita bread sign is a beauty that tops out at $400.

This Lone Rider lobby card is a $25 item. Don't confuse The Lone Rider with The Lone Ranger.

The Lone Ranger Q&A

Q: I have seen a couple of items with The _Lone Rider's_ name. Was this a real character or a mistake? Ditto, Red _Rider_. Are these misspellings?

A: The Lone Rider was a Western hero who had two lives: the U.S. version being in B-movies and the British version being a TV series, called "The Lone Star Rider. To further confuse us, Bob Livingston was among the actors who played him on the screen (he was also the second Lone Ranger of series and once played Zorro). A Lone Rider lobby card will sell for around $25, and the electric-blue Lone Star Rider Six-Gun from Brit TV sells for about $250 mint in box. The usual typo for Lone Ranger is _Long_ Ranger. Red Rider is just a generic name.

This Lone Star Rider Six-Gun is about $250 mint in box.

These Lone Ranger hardcovers sell from $125 and up.

This Lone Ranger comic is $175 item.

Look at the great artwork on The Lone Ranger Magazine. A complete run in top shape is valued at $5,000.

For $200, you could probably own these Lone Ranger pens in holster.

The Lone Ranger Airbase (shown) and box (not shown) sell for $500 for the set.

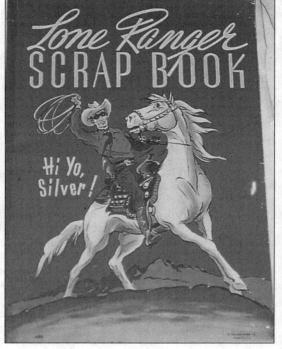

The Lone Ranger Scrap Book retails for $225.

Mandrake the Magician

38

History: Lee (The Phantom) Falk and Phil Davis co-created Mandrake in 1934. The character was on radio in two series, first in the 1930s and again from 1940-1949. A TV show survives in pilot form, and signage from the 1939 chapter play is considered highly collectible.

The Buzz: Other than big serial sheets, I've never found anything with top-dollar investibility, which is unusual for a highly collectible character who thrived in radio, comic books and strips, serial chapter, BLBs and so on.

Mandrake, Blondie, Flash, etc., Popular Comic Christmas Cards, in box, sell for $375 today.

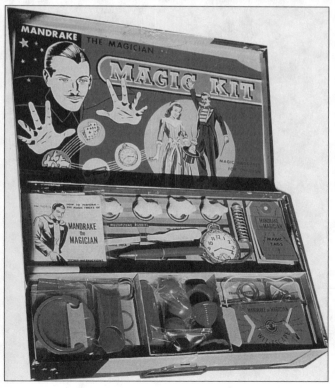

From 1949, this Mandrake Magic Kit in suitcase is a $600 item in top condition.

Rex Selections: *Mandrake the Magician*

Item	1999	2004	CF	SF	IF	TF
1. "Mandrake the Magician" 1-sheet, 1939	$1,500	$3,000	10	10	10	30
2. Mandrake Magic Kit in suitcase, 1949	$600	$1,000	10	10	10	30
* 3. Mandrake Magic Club pinback	$400	$700	10	10	10	30
4. Mandrake Tastee Bread Figural badge with letter	$400	$700	10	10	10	30
5. Mandrake the Magician in the Land of X (Feature Book #52)	$400	$800	10	10	10	30
6. Mandrake, Blondie, Flash, etc., Popular Comic Christmas Cards, in box, 1951	$375	$500	10	10	9	29
7. *Mandrake's Book of Magic* from radio series, 1944	$200	$300	10	10	9	29
8. Mandrake Christmas Card with imprint signature	$75	$100	10	9	8	27
9. Mandrake BLBs, mint, any title	$75+	$100+	10	10	7	27
10. Mandrake the Magician Coloring Book, each	$25	$40	9	8.5	7	24.5

* "Member Mandrake's Magic Club," complete with two-part membership card with the perforation intact.

Mandrake's Book of Magic is valued at $200.

This is one of many Mandrake the Magician Coloring Books, which sell for $25 each.

CF-Collectibility Factor; SF-Scarcity Factor;
IF-Investibility Factor; TF-Total Factor

Mickey Mouse

History: I've been in this collectibles thing so long that I can recall selling an original cel from "Steamboat Willie," the seminal 1928 cartoon, for less than $2,000 (I think the guy who bought it traded it in on a lakefront home!). There are no characters like the Disney gang, and Mickey is one of the two or three most famous images in the world. Floyd Gottfredson, who drew him for nearly half a century, told me there was more nonsense written about the artistic "perfection" of Mickey than could be crammed into a foot locker. All the stuff about the iconographics, the series of circles, the mystique surrounding the pie-slice eyes of the earlier mouse—Gottfredson said it was rubbish. It was just a cartoon that everybody liked. The great pieces, the books and magazines and cartoon posters, are all priced in the kazillions today. Value falls with the changing of the Golden Age Mickey Mouse to the suburban version, then into the later-day mice. In general, older is better.

The Buzz: Mice are mighty nice, but it takes a ton of that green cheese to seriously collect today. I see a couple of areas that—even as pricey as they are—strike me as undervalued.

Mouse Trivia: *Did you know that Walt Disney did not provide the original voice of Mickey on old-time ether, as is usually claimed. Radio actress Celeste Rush was the shrill voice of the rodent on "Mickey Mouse Theater of the Air," when it first broadcast in 1932. Rush's roles include that of Princess Nadji on "Chandu the Magician."*

These bisque toothbrush holders with original paint, will run about $2,500 today.

In mint, unused condition, Mickey and Donald's Race to Treasure Island Map is a $500 item.

Rex Selections: Mickey Mouse

Item	1999	2004	CF	SF	IF	TF
1. Bisque toothbrush holders, original paint, no retouch, 1930s, pair	$2,500	$3,500	10	10	10	30
* 2. Mickey and Big Bad Wolf's Race Around the Globetrotter Map	$4,500	$7,500	10	10	10	30
3. Mickey and Donald's Race to Treasure Island Map, 1939, mint, unused	$500	$800	10	10	10	30

* This item is from 1937, complete with set of pictures, pinback, a Mickey Mouse Magazine with two of the 24-picture set, in illustrated mailer (NBC, Mother's Cookies, etc.).

Mighty Mouse

History: Described by one writer as the "Murid Captain Marvel" ("Murid" referring to a family of rodents), Mighty Mouse was originally Supermouse as introduced in Terry-Toons of 1942, an obvious homage to Superman, but Mighty Mouse had a secret life apart from the comic books and cartoons. Now it can be told: Mighty Mouse was also on the radio! He was on the air, briefly, well before the an-imated cartoon series began. I'll bet you can't tell me his air name for a wheel of gouda (*Supernoodle*...a tribute to a Chicago-based radio sponsor).

When you subscribed to Terry-Toons Comics, as promoted in Issue #66, they sent the color portrait shown on this page. It is one of the rarest comic book premiums with a Total Factor of 30. This $9,000 item is solid gold, in other words.

This Mighty Mouse color portrait, a mighty rare comic book premi-um, is a mighty pricey $9,000!

History: The character of Moto was created by John T. Marquand, and it was Hollywood's way of cashing-in on the smash series about Honolulu 'tec Charlie Chan/ The top three horror stars of the 1930s—Boris Karloff, Bela Lugosi and Peter Lorre—were the respective leads in the various Moto and Mr. Wong movies, with Wong being another attempt to cash-in on Chan. Moto, Wong and Chan—it gets confusing (perhaps in the Orient, Captain Action, Captain Marvel and Captain Video are confusing!). The Lugosi Wong, for instance, was a different Mr. Wong from the others. From 1937-1939, Lorre purred his way through eight Motos. Obviously, he was moto-vated (boo, hiss, I know). Posters from the series are expensive and HTF.

The Buzz: Motos are top finds, as are the earlier Chans, but Wongs…Karloff played a rather white-looking Asian in five of the six Wongs done between 1938 and 1941, and a couple of these were quite entertaining, but two Wongs don't make a white!

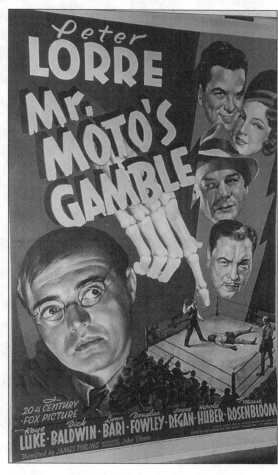

One-sheet from "Mr. Moto's Gamble." (photo courtesy of Bill Rea)

One-sheet from "Thank you, Mr. Moto." (photo courtesy of Bill Rea)

Buy it now: Moto 1-sheets, window cards, titles, anything in color and original from, especially, "Think Fast, Mr. Moto" (1937), "Thank you, Mr. Moto" (1937), and "Mr. Moto's Gamble" (1938).

Moto Trivia: *Guess where Peter Lorre was born? Who said Pittsburgh, Pennsylvania? Sorry. Transylvania? Yup, and I mean the real Transylvania.*

One-sheet from "Mr. Moto in Danger Island." (photo courtesy of Bill Rea)

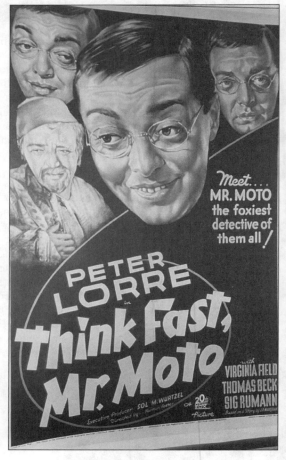

One-sheet from "Think Fast, Mr. Moto." (photo courtesy of Bill Rea)

History: Bud Fisher, cartoonist and funnyman, created Mutt & Jeff in the early-1900s. Major strip hits, they became a household synonym for any pair of two persons of different sizes, and their images appeared on scores of pins, comics and books, toys, statuettes and so on, but none of the merchandising was as well received as those hilarious strip gags.

The Buzz: Prices begin at $15 for smalls and ascend into the thousands for early toys and film posters. Mutt & Jeff also appeared in stage plays. Pieces, such as the Fisher original pen-and-ink shown on this page, still sell for under $500, and they have a secure future with a decent margin.

This Fisher original Mutt & Jeff pen-and-ink sells for less than $500, with a chance to grow in value down the road.

History: Og, Son of Fire, briefly aired in the mid-1930s radio, based on the books and stories of Irving Crump. Obscure as all get out, the character has a surprisingly large and devoted cadre of collectors, probably because of the great premiums. Libby's put out a map and a set of metal figures made by Lincoln Logs. There is something about this intriguing character that old-time radio buffs can't let go of.

The Buzz: Personally, I've been looking for 1930s radio transcriptions of the show since the late-1950s. Where did they all go? Scripts survive, and I've heard rumors of program, but I have no first-hand knowledge. You know the scripts have to be awful from that time period—lot's of grunting, groaning and screaming (imagine the WWF with a plot). Still, it would be great fun to hear one of the old shows, while tracing the action on an Og, Son of Fire Adventures Map. Alley Oop vs. T-Rex, Beyond the Valley of the Redbeards. Hoo-ha!

Buy it now: Premiums, BLBs and books. A set (by Lincoln Logs) of six metal figurines in the shipping cans, shadow-boxed in Lucite, along with a framed map qualify as a solid gold Total Factor 30! Value of this item is $2,000 today and $3,500 by 2004.

These metal figures in their original mailers are part of the $2,000 display, which includes an Og, Son of Fire Map.

This Og, Son of Fire BLB, is in poor condition and valued at $20.

History: The names are a litany: Andriola, Beck, Caniff, Raymond, Foster and Gould. For every major name that jumps instantly to mind, there are 100 brilliant comic-strip and -book artists who aren't household names but are intensely collectible. We can't all collect Frazetta and Steranko or Simon & Kirby, but at some level art is delightfully affordable to most of us. It's a great field because it remains a sub-genre where we're limited more by our eyes and taste than our deep pockets.

The Buzz: Often as not, one see fabulous potential bargains lurking in the Golden Age fields. We all know that artwork of key characters only moves in one direction (straight up, value-wise), but consider this direct quote an offering from a June 29, 1996, Sotheby's sale catalog:

Dimensional construction and painting, homage by Dan Makara, is a great value at less then $4,000. (photo courtesy of Bill Rea)

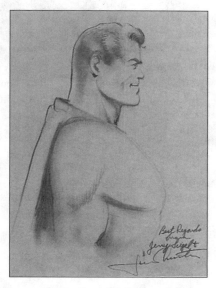

Joe Shuster/Jerry Siegel—Original drawing of Superman, graphite on paper, inscribed on lower right, "Best Regards from Jerry Siegel & Joe Shuster," excellent condition, 9-3/4 in. by 7 in., $700-$1,000. Such pieces always appear to be vastly underestimated in retrospect. (photo courtesy of Sotheby's)

Buy it now: Forget the projected values and all that stuff; instead listen to your gut instincts. What do you *love*? What can you 1) Afford and 2) Can't live without. Collecting art is simple. Ignore all outside advice (including this) and just trust your taste and instincts. The category of character-related original art is one more area that is seemingly without a marketplace ceiling. The following prices are courtesy of Christie's East from a 1994 auction. Try purchasing this same art at these prices today:

Item	Value
1. Captain America #1, recreation by Joe Simon	$6,900
2. Captain America #10, recreation by Joe Simon	$5,175
3. Showcase #4, recreation by Carmine Infantino (full color).	$4,830
4. Prince Valiant, Hal Foster, Sunday-page art	$10,925
5. Flash Gordon, Alex Raymond 1937 strip art	$8,625
6. Popeye, Segar, 1935 Sunday	$4,370
7. The Rider, Frank Frazetta	$51,750
8. Conan the Barbarian, Frank Frazetta preliminary art	$6,135
9. Dracula, Boris Vallejo's cover artwork	$9,200

10. Jack Kirby's Doctor Doom and The Silver Surfer original art sold for record prices at this sale, with the Kirby/Sinnott page from "Fantastic Four #359" (called "The Doomsday Page") setting a record for an interior Kirby, hammering down at .... $10,350.

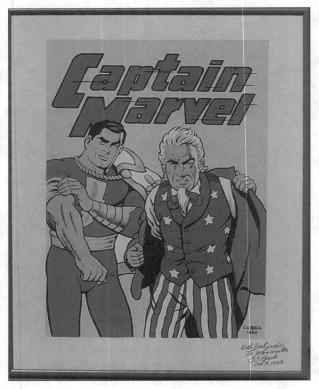

Recreation of Buck Rogers in the War with Planet Venus Better Little Book, valued at under $5,000. (photo courtesy of Marty Krim, New England Auction Gallery)

Captain Marvel and Uncle Sam recreation of comic art by C.C. Beck, is valued at under $3,000. (from collection of M. Rosenberg)

History: Lee Falk's famous achievement saw print in 1936. The Phantom, an unforgettable jungle hero dressed in purple long-johns and a black mask, sprang from the collaborative efforts of Falk and Ray Moore. Next to Batman, he's probably the least-promoted and most poorly marketed major hero character of pop culture. He was a success in strips, comics, BLBs (like his Falkian brother Mandrake) and a great wartime chapter play, but the radio show never made it. The icon of the Bandar pygmy tribe, The Ghost Who Walks, should have translated to radio wonderfully, but other than a pilot script, a hand-painted broadcast sign (for a show that may or may not have aired), it is the only evidence that the concept ever crystallized beyond the drawing board.

The Buzz: This is a *major league* player with some of the worst toys, premiums and peripheral collectibles you can imagine. Take the ring: His skull imagery should have produced a dynamite premium ring in the United States, but the closest we would come were Johnson-Smith novelty rings and a tin bend-around with his picture on it. The skull rings came out of Australia where the character still smokes, but none of them ever really hit on target...the way rings were able to capture The Green Hornet's essence, for example. Where are the keywind toys? In-store cereal box promotions (other than the Post comic rings)? Standees? Great premiums? Again, only in Australia, we find the king of Phantom collectibles—the fabulous and costly Club Member Pin. The Phantom still cooks overseas, especially in Scandinavia, but the best we can do is a ho-hum movie. Bummer! Most of the U.S.-made Phantom stuff looks like it came out of a gum machine.

The Phantom sign for radio program on WEBR is probably authentic and valued at $350.

Buy it later: Charms, plastic rings, gumballs, imitation Rolex watches, lamps...

Watch out: The Phantom Voodoo Pendant, among the nicest of all radio premium offers ain't from The Phantom. But the art deco compass ring ain't from Captain Marvel, either, so...whatever makes everybody happy, right?

Rex Selections: The Phantom

Item	1999	2004	CF	SF	IF	TF
1. "The Phantom" chapter play, 3-sheet, 1943	$7,000	$10,000	10	10	10	30
* 2. The Phantom's Club Member Pinback, Australia	$2,500	$5,000	10	11	10	31
3. The Phantom Post Ring, 1949, sealed in glassine container . . .	$350	$500	10	10	10	30
** 4. The Phantom sign for radio program on WEBR	$350	$450	10	10	9	29
5. Flashy Flickers Gun, with old film strips (Phantom, Batman, etc.)	$350	$500	10	9	10	29
6. "The Phantom" 1-sheet, 1943	$500	$800	10	9	10	29
7. The Phantom Skull Rings, stamp rings, each	$300	$450	9.5	10	9	28.5

Item	1999	2004	CF	SF	IF	TF
8. The Phantom Paint-By-Numbers set, 1967, Hasbro, sealed . . .	$300	$400	9	8	8.5	25.5
9. The Phantom Halloween mask and tunic	$250	$300	9	8	8	25
10. The Phantom pinback, several different, yellow background .	$200	$300	10	9	8	27
11. The Phantom drinking mug, grotesque!	$150	$225	8	9	9	26
12. The Phantom tab badge	$150	$250	9	8	10	27
13. The Phantom Christmas Card from Falk	$75	$125	10	9	7	26
14. The Phantom BLBs, each	$75+	$125+	10	8	9	27
15. The Phantom Rub-Ons/Magic Picture Transfers, etc., each . . .	$30	$45	10	8	9	27

* This is considered one of the 10 most beautifully designed hero collectibles.

** This is handpainted but likely authentic, ca. 1939. Similar signs exist for other old-time shows.

The Phantom Paint-By-Numbers set, 1967, from Hasbro is a $300 item in mint and sealed condition.

The Phantom's Club Member Pinback from Australia (shown in middle of this grouping) is a $2,500 rarity!

Print offer for The Phantom Skull Ring.

Print offer for The Phantom Skull Ring (stamp rings). The rings themselves sell for $300 each, with the print offers valued at $25 each.

History: Philco Vance, as you philogenists know, was created by writer S.S. Van Dine (Willard Wright) in the 1926 novel, *The Benson Murder Case*, the first of a dozen in a very popular series. Philco Vance was a combination Sherlock/Ellery-type, who would be played in early films by William Powell and Basil Rathbone. Philco remained a bankable name throughout the 1940s, in print, over radios and on screen.

"The Canary Murder Case" 1-sheet, valued at $15,000+. (photo courtesy of Butterfield & Butterfield)

This still photo from "The Dragon Murder Case" is a $20 item.

The Buzz: Vintage Philco Vance is sizzlin'! Early movie signage is sky high and is the province of advanced collectors, but you can still stumble across bargains. In recent years, a batch but restorable "Kennel Murder Case" 3-sheets turned up in somebody's garage.

My Philco Vance Wish List: I don't know if I'll ever find these items at a price I can afford, but it would be terrific to own a color card from "The Canary Murder Case." I'd settle for a poster from "The Greene Murder Case" or "The Bishop Murder Case." But what I'd really like is an original piece from "Paramount on Parade." It isn't the best movie ever made, but among the bits and sketches we see Dr. Fu Manchu (Warner Oland) do away with Sherlock (Clive Brooks) and Philco Vance (William Powell). As long as I'm wishing, I've never seen or owned any signage, premiums or whatnot from the Philco Vance radio show.

Rex Selections: Philco Vance

Item	1999	2004	CF	SF	IF	TF
* 1. "The Canary Murder Case" 1-sheet, 1929	$15,000	$20,000+	20	20	20	60!
2. "The Benson Murder Case" title card	$1,000	$1,250	10	10	10	30
** 3. Philco Vance Board Games	n/a	n/a	10	10	10	30
*** 4. Lobby and title cards from later films, each	$60+	$75+	10	10	6.5	26.5
5. Vintage original still photos with caption cut-lines	$20	$40	10	10	6	26

* The perfect mystery film sheet! Paramount cast Powell and the phenomenal beauty Louis Brooks in the first movies of the silent-to-sound-added period.

** There are three different games from the 1930s; each is valuable, but collectors fight for The Gracie Allen Murder Case and The Philco Vance Game with metal players. (See "Board Games" chapter for values.)

*** Lobby and title cards from later Vance films such as "Philco Vance Returns" and "Philco Vane's Gamble" begin in the $60-$90 range have modest Investibility of perhaps $75 to $150.

History: As recording technology and all-electric radio evolved, more or less at the same time back in the 1920s, picture records came into being. The best known series of the picture disc were made by Vogue, and they are very sought-after today, but I don't know of any that fit into the concept of "character collectibles." Radio itself spawned several interesting pieces including a very early Amos 'n Andy disc that pictured a caricature of "the boys," as they were then called. Mickey Mouse and other cartoon folk appeared on early discs, as did select radio stars. Picture discs came back into vogue (no pun intended) in the post-war 1940s, then vanished with the advent of TV.

The Buzz: These collector's items are very undervalued. Buy now!

Watch out: The Shadow Electrical Transcription Labels have been reproduced.

Rex Selections: Picture Discs

Item	1999	2004	CF	SF	IF	TF
1. Superman, two discs in color comic book-type folder, "The Flying Train," 1947.	$300	$450	10	9	10	29
2. Superman, two discs in color comic book-type folder, "The Magic Ring," 1947	$300	$450	10	9	10	29
3. Superman, serial pressbook showing these discs as suggested theatrical giveaways for chapter exhibitors	$300	$500	10	9.8	10	29.8
4. Amos 'n Andy picture record, ca. 1929.	$300	$450	10	10	9.5	29.5
5. Flash Gordon "City of Sea Caves," Terry & the Pirates "Million Dollar Baby," Red Ryder "Hermit's Gold" and Popeye set of four picture discs, Record Guild of America	$300	$450	10	9	10	29

This Superman "The Flying Train" picture disc with color comic book-type folder is a very reasonable buy at $300 today.

Flash Gordon "City of Sea Caves" from set of four picture discs, Record Guild of America. The set of four has a $300 value today, and that's great buy if you can find the set.

The reverse side of the Flash Gordon "City of Sea Caves" picture disc.

Terry & the Pirates "Million Dollar Baby" from set of four picture discs.

Red Ryder "Hermit's Gold" from set of four picture discs.

Popeye from set of four picture discs.

There are illustrated Electrical Transcription (large recordings) of Superman, The Shadow, and other top characters shown the labels. These were made by program syndicators or local stations in rare instances. This is a repro of what would be a valuable $200 Electrical Transcription, if original.

History: Although there is a record of a chapter play character referred to as Superman as early as 1920, there is no evidence to suggest he was an actual superhero. Excluding mythical figures, Popeye, one could say, was the first comic character with super powers. Lord knows how many children ate spinach in the hopes of developing huge "mus-kles" like Popeye. He was made for marketing: We all wanted pipes, figurines and anything with Wimpy on it ("I'll gladly pay you Tuesday for a hamburger today"). Popeye was an unusual character, in that his cartoon down at the neighborhood movie theater was every bit as well done as the original, which was Seager's Thimble Theater, one of the best strips ever done when it began in 1929. From the moment Popeye came upon the scene, he was a top star. His Fleischer cartoons are still as riotously funny as they were in 1933.

The Buzz: Popeye had the best store displays. A collector named Gary Greenberg has a top-flight collection of these, such as the first Thimble Theater with store display. Store toys, radio-era displays for various incarnations of Popeye sponsored by Campbell's, Popsicle, Wheatena and other companies just *kill*. All kinds of products from soup to soda to straws invoked Popeye's image. We're still unearthing examples of comic and radio series tie-ins that collectors don't know about. I recently turned up some Quaker Oats radio items from the mid-1930s.

Buy it now: You can still pick up superb Popeye collectibles without paying out truckloads of spinach (see color section for additional examples).

Displayability: One of the least valued aspects of character collectibles is the displayability factor. Let's see how this translates into saving you dollars as you collect. Take two items: A) ultra-rare Popeye Quaker Oats Diorama, a "lost" contest piece I found uncut; and B) very common Popeye Party Game:

The recently discovered Popeye Quaker Oats Diorama is a $500 find.

Rex Selections: Picture Discs

Item	1999	2004	CF	SF	IF	TF
A. Popeye Quaker Oats Diorama	$500	$1,000	10	10	10	30
B. Popeye Party Game, some of the pipes are missing, poor quality box (a hoard was dumped on the market a few years ago)	$150	$200+	10	7	6.5	23.5

If you only consider the two items as investibles, on the face, there's no comparison. The Diorama wins in each department. Let's look closer. The Party Game has a poster, which is one of the real classic pieces of pop (eye) art, with Popeye at the ship's wheel surrounded by a rope border. Cleverly mounted and framed with one of the cardboard pipes in his mouth, and with a cool double-matte or yellow frame, the beat-up game box has just doubled in value and tripled in future worth. Now consider the reason why you're collecting. Are you collecting Popeye for profit? Surely not, you're collecting be- cause you love the character. The displayability of the matted and framed poster changes the piece to a solid 10 in every respect. What might such a piece bring at a big show or convention in 2003? And the good news keeps getting better—you only paid $55.63 for the Party Game, so just by enhancing the piece's display value, you quintupled your dough. Are you smart or what? There are hundreds of Pop- eye collectibles. Use your good taste and display sense when deciding on what to buy and how much to pay, and you'll come out a winner.

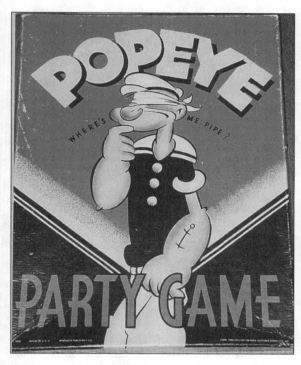

This beat up Popeye Party Game contains a great poster

This poster from the Popeye Party Game can be mat- ted and framed, enhancing the value of the low-grade game.

History: Hal Foster created a character that is unique in a couple of ways. I can think of few other heroic personas that reached such tremendous heights of popularity in a single venue, yet remained relatively unused by other media. Prince Val would seem, in retrospect, to have translated beautifully to broadcast air, but there were no adventures for him on radio. Several sword-wielders fought their way across the serial screens in Saturday chapters, but Val never made it. Small format books, Golden Age film features (a 1950s screen effort was so-so)…the areas are many to which our Prince remained an outsider.

The Buzz: Not every reader of the Sunday funnies followed Prince Valiant's exploits. He was something of an acquired taste, but if you didn't find the look of the comic strips off-putting, you'd be drawn to them instantly. Those majestic, sprawling splash panels stay in the memory forever. Sagas of imaginative high adventure, a tremendous scope and feel, the evocation of King Arthur's legend—all told through the magic of Hal Foster's special sense of wonder. It was an unforgettable look. The appeal of this character to some collectors can be summed-up in one anecdote: One Foster fan saved his money until he could afford a copy of the rare and pricey *Prince Valiant Feature Book 26*. He bought the book and carefully *dismantled* it, had each page embedded in Lucite blocks now known as "comic book fortresses," had the block drilled and fitted to a silver rod, in sequence, and then displayed them as the centerpiece of his collection.

Buy it now: This is a superfluous paragraph of you're into this character, because once you complete

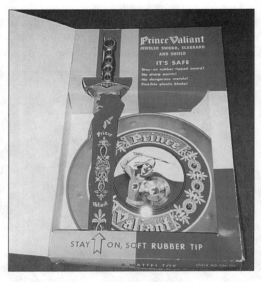

This boxed Prince Valiant Jeweled Sword, Scabbard & Shield Set is valued at $500.

your strip collection there isn't much out in the marketplace. Perhaps two-dozen *object d'art* of any significance and a few pieces like the Christmas card, transfers and pinbacks where he was lumped together with other King Features characters. Once you've picked up the crossbow sets, playset, sword and shield, the 1944 statuette, the board games, books and a half a dozen other goodies, the only thing left to do is sell the house and buy Hal Foster original art.

Rex Selections: Prince Valiant

Item	1999	2004	CF	SF	IF	TF
* 1. Prince Valiant dime-size pinback	$750	$1,500	10	10	10	30
** 2. Prince Valiant Jeweled Sword, Scabbard & Shield Set in box	$500	$850	10	10	10	30
3. Prince Valiant Castle Fort Playset, Marx, large set, #4706	$500	$750	10	9	10	29
4. Prince Valiant statuette (see color section)	$300	$450	10	9	9	28
5. Prince Valiant Crossbow Pistol Game, boxed	$250	$400	10	10	8	28
6. Prince Valiant shirt, candy premium offer	$200	$300	9	10	9	28
7. Prince Valiant Crossbow set, boxed, smaller version	$150	$225	9.5	9	9	27.5
8. Prince Valiant Halloween costume in box	$150	$250	9	10	9	28

Item	1999	2004	CF	SF	IF	TF
9. Prince Valiant Game of Valor, 1955, several similar	$125	$175	9	9	9	27
10. Prince Valiant Storybooks, each	$105	$150	9	9	8.7	25.7

* This is smaller than the 1950s pins from such sets as the one with the blue background that sells from $25-$50. This is a maroon or burgundy portrait pin and very rare. I've seen one in 30 years.

** This superb collectible has a great box with a big, displayable Foster color drawing on the back. The shield by itself is kind of weird—it looks sort of like an old Edsel hubcap, but taken as a lot this is a cool set (as is Marx's Ben Hur Double Sword, Scabbard & Shield Set.

Here is Marx's Ben Hur Jeweled Sword, Scabbard & Shield Set.

The Prince Valiant Crossbow Pistol Game, boxed, has a value of $250.

117

History: Around 1960, when character collectibles began to accelerate in value, props from old-time serials were one of the first areas to get national attention. Considering the way the hobby was still floundering at that point, it's likely that some percentage of those items might have been spurious in origin, but it marked the beginning of what would become very big business. Today, costumes and props are the focal points of auctions held by the most prestigious houses, and prices are routinely in the thousands for relatively mundane memorabilia. *Top items have a platinum future.*

The Buzz: Provenance, deep, no-nonsense documentation is a must. This is one area in which authenticity if far more important than condition. Prices, be warned, are all over the place. It's a seller's world. Sales dates follow the items listed below.

Lynda Carter's "Wonder Woman" outfit sold for more than $16,000, and is estimated to be worth $25,000 by 2004.

Batman and Robin's 1966 TV costumes sold for $23,000 in 1994. (photo courtesy of Butterfield & Butterfield)

The Batgirl outfit from Batman TV show sold for $8,625, while The Joker outfit grabbed $2,875. (photo courtesy of Butterfield & Butterfield)

This Dracula nameplate from the coffin in the original stage play has never been sold, but is estimated to be valued from $25,000-$50,000. (photo courtesy of Quantity Photo of Chicago)

Rex Selections: Props and Costumes

Item	1999	2004	CF	SF	IF	TF
1. Abbott & Costello film costumes, unspecified (1994) $3,740		$4,500	10	10	10	30
* 2. Batman and Robin's 1966 TV costumes (1994). $23,000		$35,000	10	10	11	31
3. Batgirl outfit from Batman TV show (1994). $8,625		$10,500	10	10	10	30
4. Batplane prop from 1990 film series (1997) $5,000		$7,750	10	10	10	30
5. Captain Blood velvet jacket worn by Errol Flynn (1993) . . . $31,050		??	10	10	10	30
** 6. Dracula nameplate from coffin in original stage play . . . . n/a		n/a				
7. Flash Gordon Rocket Ship prop, wooden miniature from 1938 serial (1979) $12,500		$20,000	10	10	11	31
8. Flash Gordon partial prop (Balsa, Hydrocal, etc.) from West German TV series, ca. 1954 (1979). $5,000		??	10	10	10	30
*** 9. "Gone with the Wind," Rhett Butler's ensemble worn by Clark Gable (1993) $9,775		??	10	10	10	30
10. Indiana Jones brown leather bomber jacket and brown felt hat from "Raiders of the Los Ark" (1995). $18,400		$25,500	10	10	11	31
11. Indiana Jones knapsack from "Temple of Doom" (1993). $2,590		??	10	10	10	30
**** 12. Laurel & Hardy Shriner's hat from "Sons of the Desert" $5,750		$25,500	10	10	10	30
13. The Lone Ranger, partial costume, Texas Rangers tunic worn by Clayton Moore on TV (1993) $9,200		$13,500	10	10	10	30
14. Lost in Space jumpsuits from TV series (1994) $4,025		$6,000	10	10	10	30
15. Wonder Woman costume worn by Lynda Carter on TV series. $16,100		$25,000	10	10	10	30

?? No idea as to future value

* Initial buzz on the TV show was "too campy" and that Adam West was too plump. (Holy ravioli, Batman, are you gonna be able to squeeze into those long-johns?) But the stars and show were an enormous hit.

** This in an item from the original stage play that inspired 1931 film. It was a personal gift from Bela Lugosi to the owner. It was never sold but valued from $25,000-$50,000.

*** Other similar groups went for $16,100 and $19,550.

**** I doubt if there's much immediate potential for this item, but it will go up in value. That much money being paid for a relatively minor piece of wardrobe testifies to the market strength and lasting power of such collectibles. It's still a Total Factor 30, even at this current high value.

This "Gone with the Wind," Rhett Butler ensemble worn by Clark Gable sold for nearly $10,000 (photo courtesy of Butterfield & Butterfield)

Indiana Jones brown leather bomber jacket and brown felt hat from "Raiders of the Los Ark" sold for $18,400. (photo courtesy of Butterfield & Butterfield)

History: I began answering questions for readers in the 1960s for a character collectibles column called "Premium Classics," which ran in G.B. Love's pioneer fanzine *Rocket Blast*, known as "RBCC" in collecting circles. I've been asked thousands of questions via phone, mail and in-person, through columns in antique and collectible trade paper, through my mail-order business and on radio and TV shows. This chapter is a synthesis of some of those questions.

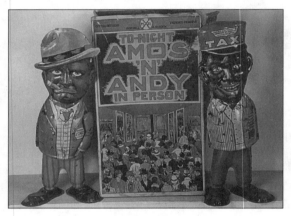

Amos 'n' Andy walking figures from Marx.

Amos 'n' Andy

Q: What are the following items currently worth? 1) Campbell's Amos 'n' Andy store sign; 2) set of cardboard stand-up figures that include the cardboard Fresh Air Taxi Cab; 3) boxed Amos 'n' Andy cartoon called "Lion Tamer"; 4) Amos 'n' Andy walking figures mint in box?

A: 1) This once-rare sign now exists in an exact repro, so not much value at present; 2) believe it or not, this Pepsodent set (the larger of the two version) just brought more than $500 at auction; 3) $75; 4) I've never found either of the two versions of this set mint in box. I know an auctioneer got about $3,000 some years back for a set with missing arms. I suppose a perfect set would sell from $5,000-$10,000.

Archies

Q: We put away some collectibles back in the 1960s, and I'm wondering what they might be worth.

A "nibbled" Archies record has little value.

I have an Archies record, a Bobby Sherman record and an Archie Club Member button. How much would you say I would get?

A: Zip-arino, I'm sorry to say. The Archies disc would be worth $150 if still left on the cereal box. Yours is cut and appears to be nibbled on. Your Bobby Sherman disc has no value as cut. Archie pinbacks are as common as lint, plus they've been reproduced and faked; unless they come with papers, they're mostly stiffs.

The Beatles

Q: We just found a flicker ring of John Lennon. I wish I had the whole set. What is this one ring worth?

A: In mint condition, it's a $25 item. You might be interested to know that a letter written by Lennon to the McCartneys sold a few years back for $90,500 at Butterfield & Butterfield. It was hand-written in black felt-tip on John and Yoko's Bag Productions, Inc., letterhead.

Q: I have a cereal box from the 1960s that has the offer for a Yellow Submarine on it. I know cereal boxes are big dollar items and The Beatles are hot, but I have never seen this listed anywhere. Can you tell me what this might be worth?

A: You didn't mention the condition, but assuming the box is complete and in excellent or better condition, I would guess in the high hundreds. I am not familiar with this box, but it sounds like a great collectible. In today's market, it might go as high as $1,500 or more.

Cap'n Crunch Island Map is a $75 item.

Cap'n Crunch

Q: I can remember a Cap'n Crunch Island Map that was way cool, from a Quaker Oats offer. Are they HTF and what are they selling for?

A: They're not difficult to find, but the price is going up. Not long ago, they were selling for $15, but I just saw one that sold for $75. This map is neat as if has the feel of the old-time radio locale maps.

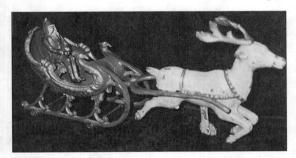

This Hubley Santa and reindeer is valued at $2,000 or more.

Cast Iron Toys

Q: I've read in a collectibles guide that cast iron toys are not hot. Is this your opinion? I sunk a lot of money into cast iron and am concerned.

A: If you love the things you bought, don't worry about it, as everything tends to move in cycles. The cast iron field has gone flat in recent years, but to say they are "not hot" implies too big of a negative. One of the hottest toys that Santa collectors want is the Hubley blue-and-gold sleigh and reindeer with the

"occult" Santa. A lot of collectors would fight for this one at $2,000.

Chapter Play Premiums

Q: I'm trying to build a collection of serial premiums but am not having much luck. I tried to purchase pins at an auction recently (Ace Drummond, Buck Rogers and The Green Hornet), but did not have a single successful bid. What's a good way to find these at reasonable prices?

A: Start with real old silent stuff that fewer collectors are interested in, like the 1914 version of "Perils of Pauline," the first version of "The Iron Claw" from 1916, "The Adventures of Ruth" and so on. Pins start as low as $20 for some of the real vintage Western and adventure titles. The more obscure, the cheaper the pin will be. You were bidding on three of the hardest-to-find pins. Some recent prices include: The Green Archer pin, 1925 version—$125; The Mysteries of Myra pin—$90 (a bargain price for this action-packed silent): Dick Tracy Shield #129, 1937—$300; The Lightning Strikes pin (unlisted serial?)—$25.

Character-Related Membership Cards

Q: I have a Junior Birdmen of America card and badge. What would you give for the pair?

A: As a dealer, I'd go $65. The gold card is HTF, but yours is beat up. The badge looks nice and the Eagle Rank would allow me to double my money.

This group of membership cards is valued at $3,000 as a lot.

This is that same group of $3,000 membership cards, but the back view.

121

Q: My friend told me there were some club cards selling for up to $1,000 each. Can this be true? Where can I find them?

A: Collectors have been slow to learn this area, and it's not too late to find bargain. Common cards now bring $50-$75 each. Cards, such as Golden Jersey Milk's The Green Hornet and the Secret Society of The Shadow are very tough to find in any shape, much less in used condition.

I'll sell you my Sky Blazer #1 comic for $300!

Col. Roscoe Tanner

Q: I've got two large store signs advertising the Col. Roscoe Tanner radio serial of the 1930s. Heinz is the sponsor. What's their value?

A: In excellent condition, they sell for around $350 and up for the pair.

Q: What is the value of the comic book, "Sky Blazers #1," in near mint condition? I've heard it goes for $300.

A: I'd sell you mine for that!

Q: I have a very rare Col. Roscoe Tanner pin from the 1930s. How much is it worth?

A: Not more than $1. You have a repro.

Davy Crockett

Q: One of my fondest childhood memories was the song, "Ballad of Davy Crockett—The King of the Wild Frontier." How would I find this song? Our local music store says it can't order it.

A: You can find the Disney records for $15-$20 each. Failing that, you might purchase a video with the theme on it.

Figurines & Statuettes

Q: I have a small pair of rubber figures from the comic strip Dick Tracy. I think they're old. What's their value?

Your figures are from a hard rubberized-plastic set issued by Marx that included Junior Tracy, Daisy Mae, Popeye and Olive Oyl, Blondie and Dagwood and so on. A complete set recently sold for the bargain price of $250. Individually, I'm afraid your figures aren't worth much, except to a completist collecting that particular image.

Q: How much is my figurine or statuette worth?

A: I get ton of these questions. I generally can't answer the ones about dolls. I miss others—even with 30 years of doing this. I didn't know the German characters "Max und Moritz," but 50 of my readers did. Many questions are about commercial trademark items such as Chiquita Banana, Mr. Peanut, Mib the Michelin Tire Man, Old Crow and so forth. Here are some examples:

This Oscar Mayer Weinermobile is an $18 item.

Q: How much is my Oscar Mayer Weinermobile worth?

A: In mint, this version is about $18.

Q: How much is my Mr. Coffee Nerves worth?

A: Ten dollars, plus the value of the frame it's in.

Q: How much is The Shadow worth?

A: That's not The Shadow, that's The Sandman who was the advertising figure for Porto Sandeman. I get "Shadow" questions all the time about figurines, decanters, signs—you name it. Some are great deco pieces and they sell well.

Q: A guy was trying to sell me a cracked Reddy Kilowatt figure for $350. Was he kidding?

A: What was it made of? Early metal and crated wood lightning bolt-body figures electrify auction bidders into paying thousands for the old Reddy Kilowatt. Reddy is a solid Total Factor 30 on my voltage meter. My advice is to pay more and get something in nice shape. If you love that particular item, buy it and get it professionally restored. This character is golden and it's getting HTF the better stuff at any prices because competition is so fierce. Smalls will eventually take off, too.

Fred Flintstone 8-inch plastic figure—$20.

Smilin' Jack plaster statuette—$75.

Q: How much is Fred Flintstone worth?
A: This 8-inch plastic item retails for $20.

Q: How much is this unpainted Smilin' Jack worth?
A: About $75 for this plaster statuette.

Woody Woodpecker ceramic figure—$75.

Michelin Man plastic figure—$25 and up.

Q: How much is Woody Woodpecker worth?
A: This ceramic version (many different) is worth $75.

Q: How much is The Michelin Man worth?
A: This plastic figure (many different) is worth $25 and up.

Willie the Penguin composition figure—$120.

The Lone Ranger carnival ashtray—$125.

Q: How much is Kool's Willie the Penguin worth?
A: This composition figure is valued at $120.

Q: How much is The Lone Ranger worth?
A: This chalkware figure on an ashtray (a.k.a., carnival ashtray) has a value of $125.

Q: What are my salt-and-pepper shakers worth?

A: The S&Ps I'm most frequently asked about are Dick Tracy and Junior (which came in a dozen or more color variations), Orphan Annie and Sandy, Don Winslow and Red, and Captain Midnight and Joyce. Typically, these sell from $100-$150. The Professional Arts Products statuettes, such as the previously mentioned Smilin' Jack statuette, the Dick Tracy lamp and the Captain Midnight figure, are harder to find and more valuable. Old figural lamps (such as Popeye) are very valuable today in original condition with shade.

This 1932 Vitagraph sheet with John Wayne in "Ride Him Cowboy" is valued in the thousands.

John Wayne

Q: I am looking for less expensive John Wayne collector's items and wonder if you have any tips.

A: Prices have gone nuts. Who would have thunk a 1932 Vitagraph sheet with John Wayne and "Duke His Devil Horse" would be trading in the thousands of dollars? I bid $11,000 for a "Stagecoach" 1-sheet and didn't even come close. Consider off-the-wall cheapies like small handbills, heralds and program throwaways. Be careful of personal items without a two-step provenance. Look for stuff no one else is seeking, such as Famous Artists Syndicate Strips, ca. 1934, of "John Wayne, Movie Star."

Junior Justice Society of America

Q: Another collector has located a World War II comic premium sendaway, from what I am told is the complete JJSOA Membership Decoder Kit from All Star Comics. He describes it has perfect, with everything, including mailing envelope. He wants $775 for it. Is it worth that much?

A: First, the decoder you showed me is from 1948-49, not WWII. However, if the kit is complete,

$775 is a bargain price for it in complete, near mint condition. It's HTF in all its many variations. The badge alone came in umpteen different materials, finishes, pin closures, etc. There are 11 pieces to the basic kit, by the way. The last mint kit I saw went for more than $1,000.

"Katzenjammer Kids #37."

"The Captain and the Kids #1."

Katzenjammer Kids

Q: I loved the Katzenjammer Kids comic strips, but I never see any collectibles except for Pep pins and Post Cereal rings. Weren't there any premiums?

A: You need to look harder! There are hundreds of Kids' goodies out there—from bottlecaps to billboards.

Krazy Kat Film Funnies and Komic Kamera.

Krazy Kat

Q: I collect old Krazy Kat comic strips, but I don't see much in American-made toys or premiums, particularly in early cast iron or tinware. What the deal?

A: The 1930s Film Funnies and Komic Kamera has Krazy Kat lithoed in color on metal. A complete set has a $550 value.

Personal items, such as this Lucille Ball studio golf cart, come up for auction occasionally.

Lucille Ball

Q: We're devoted fans of the great Lucille Ball, especially "I Love Lucy" items. Are there any special things we should keep an eye out for?

A: Personal Lucille Ball memorabilia does get to the marketplace now and again. Her pale blue studio golf cart went for $8,050.

Masked Man

Q: Who was the masked man...and what do they have in common? Here's a clue: Bert Lytell, Henry Walthall, Bertram Grassby, Jack Holt, Thomas Meighan, Melvyn Douglas, Francis Lederer, Warren William, Gerald Mohr, Ron Randell and Louis Hayward all played this character on screen. Here's another clue: The <u>nature</u> of the character changed from picture to picture, but he was always a kind of wolf. You've got it! The Lone Wolf (or Michael Laynard) was in 25 feature films and a TV series, as well as an old-time radio show. Collectibility and Scarcity Factors of Lone Wolf's silent-movie paper is high, but the Investibilty Factor is disproportionately low.

Old-Time Radio

Q: At a local flea market, I chanced upon what I think is a very scarce pin from the old radio series "Dimension X." What is its value?

A: It's a contemporary piece from a recent comic book kit, privately produced.

Lum and Abner Walkin' Weather Prophet.

Q: I have a Lum and Abner badge that is supposed to predict the weather, but it never changes color. Does this diminish the value?

A: No. The litmus inserts for such premiums as Captain Diamond Weather Predictor and The Lone Ranger Weather Predictor Ring, were made by impregnating stock inserts with calcium chloride solution, which oxidized over time.

Weird Tales contained stories of "The Witch's Tale."

Q: Is there anything collectible from "The Witch's Tale?" I've been told there is a blotter.

A: Yes, and a matchbook. Also, *Weird Tales* carried the stories.

"Land of the Lost #5" from EC Comics.

Q: I've been trying to find collectibles from a ju-

125

venile show called "Land of the Lost." What kinds of premiums were available?

A: First, "Land of the Lost" was a post-war kid show unrelated to the program on TV. The sponsor, Bosco, offered "Oh-fish-ul Red Snapper Membership Pins" which seem to have vanished. A run of appealing EC Comics can still be found at 25% of their potential value.

Alka-Seltzer "Barn Dance" premium. The item says, "Set this Alka-Seltzer Barn Dance on or near your radio and you will get more pleasure and enjoyment from this popular radio program every Saturday night."

Half-sheet for "David Harding, Counterspy" sells for a measly $12.

This movie sheet for "Fibber McGee and Molly" is bargain priced today.

Consider purchasing movie sheets featuring radio show turned into films, such as "Suspense," as the prices are right for collectors.

Q: Why didn't old-time radio mysteries offer many premiums?

A: The shows were targeted toward adults, so the giveaways tended to be money, cars and other things grown-ups wanted. Sometimes, programs like "House of Mystery" would offer kid stuff, but for every show like "David Harding, Counterspy" that issued some children's premiums through its Pepsi-Cola tie-in, there were several programs like "I Love a Mystery" without sponsor sendaways.

Some examples of radio programs that offered hardware premiums of interest were soaps like "David Harum," who sent out an aerial view of Homeville with a Mystery Handprint from Babo. "The Romance of Helen Trent" made radio-shaped TV pins and medallions available. Hardware from shows like "Girl Alone" and "Just Plain Bill" have yet to show signs of heating up, but I predict the embers will start smoking as more time passes. Premiums pop up for variously formatted shows, such as badges from the cornball comedy mystery of the early-1930s, "Detectives in Black and Blue," juveniles such as "That Brewster Boy" and "Dick Steel, Boy Reporter," Oxydol's "Ma Perkins," Johnson Wax's "Fibber McGee and Molly," and Alka-Seltzer's "Barn Dance."

Posters from films based on old radio shows have yet to take off in value. If you're having trouble finding display collectibles from vintage favorites, consider this untapped field. For example, a half-sheet for "David Harding, Counterspy" is currently selling for $12!

Our Gang

Q: My wife is a devoted fan of the "Our Gang" and the "Little Rascals" comedies. Anything with Alfalfa, Spanky, etc., by way of collectibles, we'd be interested to know about.

A: There are tons of smalls and papergoods. Prices range from $12-$15 for a $4,000 set that included painted statuettes, a stage similar to the Tarzan in Jungleland premium and a set of china nodders.

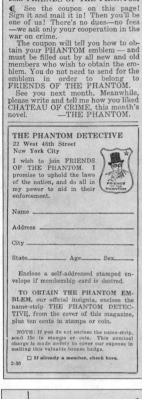

Friends of The Phantom Club Card membership offer.

Friends of The Phantom Club Card.

The Phantom (Detective)

Q: A San Diego collector says he purchased a lapel badge and membership card, both scarce premiums, from the 1930s Friends of The Phantom Club, but was disappointed to learn they weren't from THE Phantom. The dealer who sold the set advertised it as a Phantom emblem and Friends of The Phantom Club Card, but the collector says it's from

the pulp character The Phantom Detective. Who is correct?

A: You both are! The pulp called its character "The Phantom" as much as it did by his full name, "The Phantom Detective." In any case, the 10 cents sent back in 1936 appreciated by around $1,000 if you held on to your bright red club card and metal emblem that came in the mail.

Tarzan pop-up.

Buck pop-up.

Flash pop-up.

Pop-Up Books

Q: I have a rare pop-up book called The Pop-Up Flash Gordon in Tournament of Death. I also have a pop-up from The Pop-Up Buck Rogers Strange Adventures in the Spider Ship (I don't have the book itself, but the pop-up is in mint condition. Can you tell me what these two items are worth?

A: The Flash Gordon book is about $500 in the condition yours is in, which is excellent or better. Other books in this series, (Tarzan, Buck, Terry) with the pop-ups intact and in pristine condition sell from $500-$750 each. I have no clue what you might ask for the single pop-up. I'd just offer it to the highest bidder.

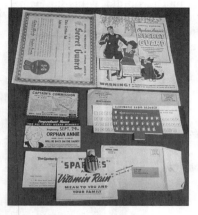

Little Orphan Annie Secret Guard Kit.

Radio's Little Orphan Annie

Q: Can you tell me about Orphan Annie's Secret Guard. I have a couple of decoders from the show and I'd like to know the values. Mine are mint.

A: Completeness is a factor. Shown in a typical Secret Guard kit with all the goodies, mailers, papers, etc. It's $450 as you see it. The two decoders from the wartime years are not easy to find. Many dealers find a big kit like the one shown and break it up into pieces to get more money out of it. There's no law against it, but it really sucks, if you ask me. Captain Sparks, shown with Annie on the paperwork from these 1940-42 items, was Quaker's answer to Captain Midnight, and Captain Sparks really sucked.

Roadrunner

Q: I love the Roadrunner and Coyote cartoons. When I see anything to collect from the Roadrunner, it's always overpriced for my budget. Are there some cute collectibles that can still be called inexpensive?

A: Sure. The set of six glasses Pepsi-Cola gave away in 1973 would be a current bargain. You could buy a Roadrunner glass for about $20, or the whole set (Roadrunner, Bugs, Sylvester, Tweety, Daffy and Porky) for $100, if you're lucky. I foresee this set tripling in value in the coming years. I'd also look for the movable figures. An 8-inch Roadrunner can still be found from $35-$40. *Meep-meep! Pppeww!*

Sgt. Preston

Q: I have a land deed from Sgt. Preston of the Yukon to a square-inch of land in goldrush country. What is it worth?

A: I have been asked this hundreds of times. Not much, is the answer, because a horde of thousands of sequential deeds were dumped into the marketplace and the value plunged from $35 to zilch. This was a great promotion by Quaker's in 1955, on radio, TV and print. It was an idea first used in a turn-of-the-century promotion, again by Amos 'n' Andy radio sponsor in 1930 and others, but it suited "Challenge the Yukon" to perfection. It made fun of itself and played to our greed at the same time—a perfect something-for-nothing concept. By the way, the deeds are now selling for around $20 each.

Who is that thin man on the cover of The Thin Man *1934 hardcover? It's Dashiell Hammett. This hardcover is a $350 item.*

The Thin Man

Q: We collect "The Thin Man" movies and TV shows. The posters are too expensive. Are there any radio premiums or toys?

A: No, not much. I suggest magazines as a source for inexpensive items. A TV guide with Nick and Nora Charles on the cover is $30 or so. A cereal ad from the radio show is $15. A handbill is $35. A 1934 herald, fairly scarce and frameable, went for $75. An original script is less than $20. A Grossett & Dunlap hardcover with black-mask interior is $350, if you can go that high. It's interesting that *a* thin man is show on the photo dust jacket, and as you realize that *the* Thin Man was not Nick Charles but just a peripheral character in the first novel. The skinny gent on the book cover is Dash Hammett!

3-D

Q: I'm trying to build a collection of material on the 3-D process and have been fortunate to find House of Wax, Mighty Mouse, The Three Stooges

This ad for Pete Smith's 3-D Murder is a frameable item that retails for $30.

and The Creature items. I'm looking for more. The only problem is when I find it, it is too pricey.

A: A lot of collectors are interested in every aspect of 3-D, from glasses to comic books. Try the offbeat stuff nobody else looks for.

TV Adventure Shows

Q: I was a big fan of the Irwin Allen shows from the mid-1960s ("Lost in Space" and "T.H.E. Cat"). I've seen a board game for T.H.E. Cat, but nothing else. Do episodes of the program survive?

A: About a dozen or so of T.H.E. Cat programs are floating around in videophiles' collections. Here are a few goodies from that period to look for:

1. Lost in Space Playset from Mattel, sealed and mint, it has gone as high as four figures.
2. Lost in Space robots. These vary in value. A Remco 'bot from 1966 has sold from $400-$700. Others have been made in later years for lesser dough.
3. Lost in Space runs the price gamut. You can spend $2 for a paperback or $2,000 for a Lost in Space gum display box with two dozen sealed packs from 1966. I just paid $10 a

stack for Gold Key Comics of "Lost in Space," Voyage to the Bottom of the Sea," "Sea Hunt," "Rat Patrol," and so on. They're all 12-cent comics from the mid-1960s.

4. T.H.E. Cat window-boxed gun set with a cap-buster, plastic stiletto with sheath, ID, ring, etc., from Ideal is a probably four-figure item mint in unopened box.

What's It Worth?

1. Amos 'n' Andy and Double Check 1930 color movie herald—$80
2. Bing Crosby cover issue of radio magazine—$10
3. Captain Frank Hawkes Sky Patrol Badge—$25
4. Dick Tracy World War II postcard (for member armed forces)—$12.50
5. Esther Williams photo with imprint signature—$5
6. Fibber McGee and Molly recipe booklets from radio, three different, all—$35
7. Gene Autry color photo from Melody Ranch Show, in mailer—$100
8. Gene Autry b&w photo with Melody Ranch letter—$70
9. Huckleberry Hound ring, unused, brass, TV premium—$250
10. Inner Sanctum blotter—$10
11. Jean Hersholt/Dr. Christian Wrigley's b&w photo—$4
12. Katy Keene dolls cut-outs in premium mailer, uncut—$55
13. The Lone Ranger Card with contest for coloring, General Mills—$30
14. Marilyn Monroe 8 x 10 original color still, Fox Studios, 1949—$15
15. Nelson Eddy/Jeanette MacDonald sheet music, posed inside heart—$10
16. Orphan Annie Treasure Hunt Game, unused in mailer, with boats—$185
17. Omar the Mystic club pin—$30
18. Quiz Kids, red/black/white pinback—$10
19. Roy Rogers Riders coin, card, photo with mailer, 1949, by Rohr—$200
20. Sky King Magic Kit with Peter Pan radio card, in mailer—$125
21. Terry & the Pirates, six-picture contest postcard, color—$45
22. Uncle Wiggily 1920s children's book—$30
23. Vic and Sade Crisco Map in mailer—$350
24. Wonder Woman 1970s Nestles ring—$30
25. Zorro 1959 Canada Dry pinback—$1

History: The highly identifiable likeness of the red-haired cowpoke in the white hat was created in 1938 by Western artist Fred Harmon, whose original art sells in the low- to mid-five figures. Strip comic books, BLBs, hardcover books, specialty publications, dozens of movie features and a serial, as well as a variety of radio and TV incarnations chronicled the exploits of hard-ridin' Red and his Navajo buddy Little Beaver.

The Buzz: For a top character, we find few store items. His major marketing tie-in was with Daisy, which found him to be an unparalleled salesman of B-B carbines—you can still buy them 60 years later! The acquisition of a Red Ryder B-B-Firing Cowboy Carbine, complete with rawhide thong to tie your lucky coin or arrowhead on to, was the goal of every boy who grew up in the late-1940s. Red is one of the few heroic images whose feature paper is more sought-out than his serial posters. There were a couple of confusing identity matters involving the names of the actors who played Red on screen. Don "Red" Barry, an actor who starred in the "Adventures of Red Ryder" chapter play in 1940, was confused with Red Barry, the detective hero. "Wild Bill" William Elliott, whose second film career has been boosted by his successful portrayal of Wild Bill Hickok, was also the primary Red Ryder in the 1940s B-Westerns. Kids who saw his posters at the Bijou and expected to see a Red Ryder show were sometimes disappointed. But we got over it.

Ad for Red Ryder Golden Banded 1000-Shot Saddle Carbine.

Mailer for Red Ryder WWII Victory Patrol Membership Kit.

Red Ryder 18 x 12-inch Republic Pictures ad is a $200 piece.

Rex Selections: Red Ryder

Item	1999	2004	CF	SF	IF	TF
1. Red Ryder Golden Banded 1000-Shot Saddle Carbine with Daisy Air Rifles Catalog, Christmas Reminder sendaway and original Harmon-illustrated box, 1940	$1,750	$3,000	10	10	10	30
2. Red Ryder prop, giant book	$5,000	$10,000	10	10	11	31
3. Red Ryder WWII Victory Patrol Membership Kit with Super Book of Comics in self-contained mailing unit	$1,000	$2,000	10	10	10	30
4. Red Ryder Target Game with balls and catapult, 1939	$400	$500	10	10	9	29
5. Red Ryder Rodeomatic Radio Decoder from Victory Patrol	$400	$500	10	10	9	29
6. Red Ryder Membership Card from Radio Patrol	$400	$500	10	10	9	29
7. Red Ryder Daisy Catalogs, group of three	$400	$500	10	10	9	29
8. Lot of four items: Victory Patrol Badge ($150), Penney Lucky Coin ($20), "I have entered the Red Ryder Pony Contest" pin ($35), pinback from Red/Little Beaver set ($100)	$305	$400	10	9	9	28
9. Little Beaver pin, yellow background	$75	$100	10	9	8	27
10. Red Ryder gloves, pair, no box	$75	$100	10	9	8	27
11. Red Ryder Silver Star, various imprints, each	$75+	$100+	10	9	8.5	27.5
12. Red Ryder 18 x 12-inch ad for features, Republic Pictures	$200	$300	8	10	9	27
13. Red Ryder 1-sheet, "Conquest of Cheyenne"	$175	$225	8	9	9	26
14. Red Ryder Molding set with rubber molds in original box	$175	$225	8	8	8	24
15. "Adventures of Red Ryder," title card from serial	$175	$225	9	10	8	27

Super Book of Comics from Red Ryder WWII Victory Patrol Membership Kit.

In the background of this photo, you can see the Red Ryder prop, giant book, which is valued at $5,000.

This Red Ryder Target Game is a $400 item.

Official Membership Certificate/ Secret Decoder from Red Ryder WWII Victory Patrol Membership Kit.

Tremendous bargains can still be found today in premium rings, even at the best-publicized venues. Several of the above prices-realized were hammered down at Sotheby's June 17, 1995, premium auction. At that same event, some bidder picked up seven Sky King radio rings, including the scarce Aztec Calendar Ring for $977, which translates into getting six rings free. I paid nearly $39,000 for a rare pair of Superman rings that same year, buying on behalf of a client, in an Auctions Unlimited sale.

As a collector said of the Radio Orphan Annie Altascope Ring, which sold for around $13,000 at the Sotheby's sale—why? The answer is simple—because! That's why. 1995's apparent lunacy seems like good sense only a few years later. What will 2004 bring? Tune in tomorrow. And bring a bucket of money.

The future of rings: It's anybody's guess. No one knows for sure what prices will be on this super-expensive premium memorabilia in 2004. Some rings seem to be incredible bargains. A Woody Woodpecker 1958 Secret Code Ring and cereal box flat with a Rice Krispies sendaway sold for only $150 for the lot. If that ain't 30 on the Woody meter, what is? I could estimate the value of the Woody lot at $800 for 2004. Wish we had a deal like that on certificates of deposit.

Rings: Absolute 10s

Ring	Prices realized in 1995
1. Buck Rogers Luminous Ring with Manual	$1,800
2. Captain Midnight Mystic Sun-God Ring with Manual	$4,200
3. Don Winslow Squadron of Peace Ring	$3,735
4. Frank Buck, two rings as a lot	$6,325
5. The Green Hornet Secret Seal Ring	$3,450

One of the two rare Superman rings that the author paid $39,000 for in 1995.

One view of the front of one of the two rare Superman rings that sold for $39,000.

Another view of the front of the rare Superman ring.

Buy it now: Here are some undervalued rings that have yet to catch fire:

1. Captain Midnight Skelly Ring with red checkmark.
2. Andy Pafko Baseball Scorekeeper Ring from Muffetts.
3. Superman Silver Crusader Ring—this Kellogg's premium is already starting to become scarce in uncirculated mint.
4. "Roger Wilco" glowing Magni-Ray with insert paper in secret top. This green-glowing ring was offered on some radio programs of the 1940s, perhaps Hop Harrigan, but, due to licensing, the sponsor issued rings as "Roger Wilco," a nonexistent aviator in the same manner of Captain Sparks for Quaker's. Children of the day played with it as a Green Lantern ring, because of its JJSA-type shield markings, and the fact that it functioned as a "Green Lantern Power Ring," which was never marketed. The Roger Wilco rings are still findable for around $300, and they have $1,000 futures.

History: Robin was created for Detective Comics #38 in 1940. He was the perfect sidekick. He held Batman's cape, as it were, in countless adventures in print, over radio and TV, in two 1940s chapter plays and movies that have proved to be box-office blockbusters half a century later. He's among that handful of superstars whose rarest memorabilia would seem to have no market maximums.

The Buzz: Top-of-the-line goods will go straight up! Concentrate on Golden, Silver Age and mid-1960s merch. Anything with The Boy Wonder is solid platinum and the supply dwindles as we speak. Best bets: key and first-issue comics, serial signage, unusual 1940s stuff like trading cards, top TV-era goodies like bookends and premium posters—it's all money in el banko.

Buy it now: Wartime period specialty signage or art, such as war bonds, war stamps, March of Dimes-type advertiques or original art—if you can afford it.

Watch out: Be advised that those of us who lust for a Robin Secret Code Maker need to know that the radio premium is unrelated to *that* Robin.

Detective Comics #38. (photo courtesy of Christie's East)

Robin premium poster with caption.

Robin trade card with 1949 set.

Rex Selections: Robin

Item	1999	2004	CF	SF	IF	TF
* 1. Detective Comics #38.	n/a	n/a	-	-	-	-
2. Robin premium poster with caption (see "Batman" chapter), pair	$400	$750	10	9	10	29
3. Robin trade card with 1949 set	$400	$750	10	10	10	30
4. Robin key and special comic issues, i.e., "Star Spangled Comic" in which Robin battles a clock	$400	$750	10	9	10	29

* If you have to ask the price, you can't afford it. If you can afford it, you don't care what it will be worth in 2004. Today the car, tomorrow the farm.

History: Roy Rogers (RR), King of the Cowboys from the late-1930s on, is part of pop culture. He rode Trigger across the screen in countless oaters, radio adventures and in a long-running TV series. Most kids would could tolerate singing cowboys were firmly in either Roy's or Gene's camp. The name "Roy Rogers" was half-forgotten by younger folks when music producer Snuff Garrett, famous for his Nostalgia Merchant hobby/business, brought

Roy Rogers toy guns from the Kilgore Deluxe Guns and Holster Set.

The classic Roy Rogers still photo. Compare Roy's real six-guns with the Kilgore set.

Rogers back in the limelight with the poignant hit recording "Hoppy, Gene and Me." Roy Rogers is the top character in Western collecting, even before his passing in 1998 (which of course drew more attention to Roy and his memorabilia).

The Buzz: Deluxe cap gun sets, store standees and boxed toys—mint store stock in particular—has been selling for thousands of dollars in recent years. These things will remain smokin' hot. The top of the collectible gun sets is the RR Double Holster and Gun Set from Kilgore. It features a big golden buckle with bas relief images of Roy and Trigger, a 6-1/2-inch wide double-belted holster rig in honey pine,

cartridges and belt with Roy's name, and beautifully designed 10-1/2-inch swing-out cylinder guns in ornate silver. Boxed guns sets of all kinds are now sky high.

Buy it now: Don't overlook a bargain area of Roy Rogers goodies. Put together things such as the microscope or branding iron ring with the strip ad for it, the souvenir mug with the store sign, the RR Riders Kit with the full newspaper page, the RR Cookies Pop Gun with color offer, and you double the value invested almost instantly. Any premium or giveaway with the mint cereal box is solid platinum.

A Roy Rogers Dream Collection: A bunkhouse room in rustic cedar or knotty pine filled with RR items: framed rodeo sign ($475), real cowboy gear

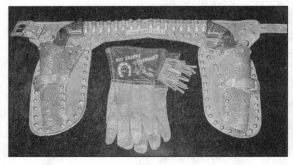

Roy Rogers Schmidt Double Gun and Holster Set ($975), with Roy Rogers & Trigger fringed gloves ($120).

(spurs, six-guns and a lasso), boxed RR guitar ($175), complete boxed outfit or child's mannequin attired in RR stuff, and an RR lantern ($175) to illuminate the scene. Sound good? Better start putting it together now!

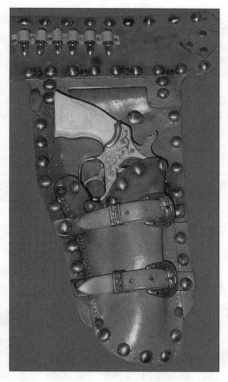

Roy Rogers Kilgore gun in a holster.

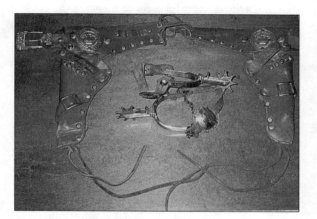

Roy Rogers Double Holster Set and Spurs is a $780 set.

This Roy Rogers strip ad for his cookies is a $40 item.

Roy Rogers Stopped His Horse

This Irwin Hess original BLB art will run you $250.

Rex Selections: Roy Rogers

Item	1999	2004	CF	SF	IF	TF
1. RR life-size articulated standee with glow-in-the-dark trick lasso, one of two similar signs, this one has the glowing lasso included.	$2,400	$4,000	10	10	10	30
2. RR Kilgore Deluxe Guns and Holster Set	$2,250	$3,500	10	10	10	30

Item	1999	2004	CF	SF	IF	TF
3. RR souvenir cup display, with sign, mounted strip offer with premium, cup in cardboard stand, Quaker's round cereal box and a three-part display for an identical Quaker Man offer, seven items in all	$2,000	$3,000	10	10	10	30
4. "Under Western Stars" 1-sheet	$1,100	$2,250	10	10	10	30
5. RR Schmidt Double Gun and Holster Set	$975	$1,500	10	10	10	30
6. RR Double Holster Set and Spurs without guns	$780	$1,200	10	10	9	29
* 7. RR Cookies store sign, ad and pop gun, three pieces in all	$400	$750	10	10	9	29
8. Lot of four BLBs, plus BLB art (art is $250 by itself)	$450	$700	10	10	9	29
9. RR rubber knife in riveted sheath	$150	$275	10	10	9	29
10. Roy Rogers & Trigger fringed gloves	$120	$225	10	10	9	29

* Strip ad is about $40 by itself.

**CF-Collectibility Factor; SF-Scarcity Factor;
IF-Investibility Factor; TF-Total Factor**

Roy Rogers Cookies cardboard pop-gun.

*Roy Rogers rubber knife in riveted
sheath is a $150 item.*

History: Sam Spade, Philip Marlowe and, years later, Mike Hammer, were three of the hardest of the hard-boiled eggs in detective fiction. Their origins were from print medium. Dashiell Hammett, who created Spade in the 1920s, and Raymond Chandler, whose worked spawned Philip Marlowe, were the co-fathers of what became known as pulp fiction, at least where tough 'tecs were concerned. Their forum was a woodpulp mystery called "Black Mask," which nurtured the likes of Erle Stanley Gardner, Cornell Woolrich, James M. Cain and the you John D. McDonald. (Mickey Spillane came out of the comics, and his phenomenal *I, The Jury* was single-handedly responsible for the era of paperback novels), but of all these writer's creations, Hammett's Spade was unique. Modeled on Hammett's own experience as an agent for "Pinks," he was the prototype for the characters who would follow, especially on film.

The Buzz: There are only a few Sam Spade collectibles and most are priced beyond the reach of mainstream hobbyists. A complete quintet of the first five Black Masks containing "The Maltese Falcon," which ran from September 1929 to January 1930, sold for $25,000 some years ago. Original signage from the 1941 (third) version of the book filmed, is the most sought-after film *noir* movie paper. Few categories can boast a more ardent or cultish following in the realm of populist entertainment than the genre of *noir* in general, Spade in particular.

Buy it now: The most undervalued area of Spade collectibles is in the first (1931) filmic treatment of

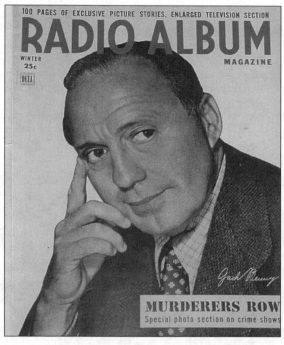

Cover of Radio Album Magazine with Sam Spade article, has a $25 value.

Falcon, a.k.a., "Dangerous Female," with Ricardo Cortez. Dated and stagy, it actually comes closer in some respects to being true to Hammett's vision of the book than the extraordinary remake by John

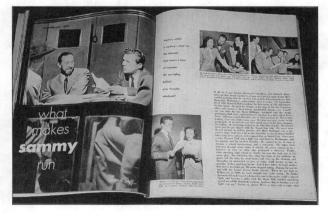

Inside of Radio Album Magazine.

Huston. Also look for oddball original pieces such as Wildroot radio ads, playing cards, radio magazines, etc. "The Maltese Falcon" color cards will set you back anywhere from $1,500 and up, if you can find one for sale.

Buy it later: Mock-ups of The Maltese Falcon statue, poster repros (which have been sold by the kazillion for years in every size from postcard to life-size standees) and hardcovers without dust jackets.

Watch out: Props have been sold with questionable provenance.

Rex Selections: Sam Spade

Item	1999	2004	CF	SF	IF	TF
1. Deluxe 1931 presskit, super bargain	$110	$400	10	10	10	30
2. "Tune In Adventures of Sam Space" on ace of spades playing card, scarce radio-era item, ca. 1946, station specific . . .	$150	$300	10	10	10	30
3. "Adventures of Sam Space," set of 4 Wildroot Creme Oil comic strip ads in color, for all 4	$100	$200	10	10	9	29
4. *Radio Album Magazine*, 1948, rare picture story on Sam Spade	$25	$100	10	10	9	29
5. Howard Duff, autographed photo from Sam Spade program . . .	$35	$100	10	10	8	28

"The Maltese Falcon" color card is valued at $1,500+.

History: Secret agents have been around as long as man has waged covert warfare, which means forever. With the strengthening of commercial broadcasting, ca. 1929, the dramatic and adventure programs starting mining the secret-agent world for plots and heroes. The early shows, such as "Secret Agent K-7" and "Secret Agent K-7 Returns" had many sponsors and premiums. In strips, there was "X-9" and "Red Barry," both of whom would go on to star in various print and air media and on the serial screen. By the time of the nostalgia explosion in the 1960s, these characters were mostly forgotten, as James Bond books, the favorites of JFK, were made into smashingly good pictures with Shawn Connery as 007. Shows like "The Man from U.N.C.L.E." (Napoleon Solo was named by Ian Fleming) and "Danger Man" were big on TV, and Johnny Rivers' song "Secret Agent Man" topped the charts. All these characters went flat with the end of the Cold War: The wall came down and SMERSH went squish.

The Buzz: As investibles, Secret Agent X-9, Hammett's character, has some currency, as does Bond and some of the TV stuff, but these things have fallen mostly in the hands of completists. Peripheral programs such as "Wild Wild West" are actually hotter now.

Buy it now: Secret Service stuff is way underpriced: An unused mint-in-the-box Kilgore Gun and Holster Set sold for $80; Secret Service Boy Operative Shield, $35; Secret Service badge, $15; Sunkist Secret Service Shield, $30; FBI Secret Agent Shield and Secret Periscope shaped like a Cracker Jack box mint in original container, $65 as a lot.

This Secret 6 Manual of Secret Tricks is an $18 item.

Rex Selections: Secret Agents

Item	1999	2004	CF	SF	IF	TF
New Age Agentry						
* 1. James Bond 007 Attaché Case, 1965, complete/unused in box	$1,000+	$1,200+	10	10	10	30
2. James Bond 007 Corgi Aston-Martin in display box, accessories	$400	$500	9	9	9	27
3. James Bond Villain Odd Job action figure, 1965	$250	$350	9	9	9	27
** 4. Man from U.N.C.L.E. Secret Service Gun, 1965, accessories	$750	$900	9	9	9	27
*** 5. Man from U.N.C.L.E. Napoleon Solo Slush Metal Gun Kit	$1,500	$1,750	9	9	9	27
Golden Age Agentry						
6. Secret Agent 4 "Leader" pinback	$75	$100	10	10	8	28
7. Secret 3 Kit, manual, badge and "burn" letter	$110	$150	9	10	8.5	26.5
8. Secret 6 Manual of Secret Tricks	$18	$30	8	9.2	8	25.2
9. Secret Agent K-7 Club Shield, several different, each	$35	$45	8	9	8	25
10. Secret Agent X-9 Silver Shield with scarce card	$125	$170	10	10	8	28

* Everybody wanted the shooting attaché case with concealed dagger, scoped rifle and all the spy goodies from the movie, right down to the latch-controlled self-destruct feature.

** Accessories to this Ideal toy include holster, silver ID, triangle badge in window box.

*** This scarce 1965 kit includes working receiver, insertable magazine, screw-on threaded supporter and flash-hider, detachable scope and shoulder stock.

History: Among the first broadcast properties with adventure themes were stories of the Royal Canadian Mounted Police, like "Blair of the Mounties" and "King of the Royal Mounted." The show "Challenge of the Yukon" was George W. Trendle's attempt to follow the success of The Lone Ranger and The Green Hornet, but this time with a non-masked hero. Instead of Tonto or Kato, a dog—Yukon King—was the sidekick. The concept worked, but it would be nearly a decade before a major network picked up the kid's show in the post-war 1940s. From the second we heard the William Tell Overture/Flight of the Bumblebee and Preston's authoritative "On King! On you huskies!" we were firmly hooked. Quaker's got tremendous mileage from the show that was "shot from guns."

The Buzz: There are tons of premiums to collect, from tents to police whistles, but the big three goodies are the pinbacks, the Yukon Trail and the 10-in-1 Electric Trail Kit, each of which has fetched $2,500-$5,000 on at least one occasion.

Buy it now: Anything related to the "Hunt for Gold" theme, the strong sub-theme of the radio and TV shows: Prospector Kits, Gold Ore Detectors, Trail Kits and Pedometers, Signal Flashlights, Leatherette Pouches full of Klondike Land, Fool's Gold and, of course, Preston-related cereal boxes.

Buy it later: Deeds without mailers. The piggy-back/bounce-back offers are far more valuable than the deeds themselves because so many exist numerically.

Sgt. Preston wish list: Challenge of the Yukon "Hunt for Gold" goodies: Prospector's Pouch with

Print ad for Prospector's Pouch, 1 oz. Of Klondike Land and Deed.

fool's gold samples (iron pyrite), Prospector's Pouch in unused condition with print offer, Goldrush-area Klondike Big-Inch Deed in envelope from Richard Simmons (who was Preston at the time of the offer), Map of Yukon Goldrush Territory, Electronic Gold Ore Detector in mailer and complete, Sgt. Preston and King color card, Sgt. Preston's 10-in-1 Electric Trail Kit with print offers in b&w and color. All of these items are valued at around $3,500 today and $4,500 in 2003, with a Total Factor score of 31!

Rex Selections: Sgt. Preston

Item	1999	2004	CF	SF	IF	TF
* 1. Sgt. Preston and King poster, large.	$1,250+	$1,500+	10	10	10	30
2. Autographed photo of Paul Sutton, rare, be sure to get in mailer.	$400	$600	10	10	10	30
3. Sgt. Preston store display, cereal box and whistle with lanyard	$800	$1,100	10	10	10	30
4. Sgt. Preston on Rex the Wonder Horse, with accessories	$200	$300	10	9	9	28
5. St. Preston tent, unused	$350+	$450+	10	10	8	28

* This beautiful full-color artwork piece comes in three sizes, the larger wall posters being a contest prize from around 1950, the smallest being a postcard. The big one in the tube is a super premium.

Print ad for Electronic Ore Detector.

Print ad for 10-in-1 Electric Trail Kit.

Several Challenge of the Yukon "Hunt for Gold" goodies.

History: *Who knows...what evil...lurks.* If you heard it then, you can still hear it now—that sinister, loaded-with-payback resonance, followed by a chilling cackle of crazed laughter. The Shadow epitomized both vintage radio and the world of pulps. There were two slightly different Shadows, but they played perfectly in counterpoint, leading their parallel lives on the air and in print throughout the Golden Age. Only a couple of super-heroic personas have achieved loftier plateaus in collecting circles. His merchandise, premiums, pulps, posters, BLBs, artwork, whatever—plays in the same arena with Superman, Batman, Captain Marvel, Tarzan, Buck and a few others. *The Shadow knows!*

The Buzz: Boxed games, premiums in mailers, the key pulp mags—this is all hard stuff to find in any condition, but in mint grade? Jeepers. And when is comes to the major pieces such as a 1-sheet or 3-sheet from the 1940 Victory Jory serial, The Shadow items become ultra-difficult to pursue. There isn't much to go around, and the competition for the meager supply is fierce. Dedication, more than discretionary income, is what it takes to find these treasures. You'd better be some kind of hunter.

Buy it now: There are spectacular things to collect (see color section), but my advice to someone looking to build a great Shadow collection would be to think in terms of displayability rather than top pieces. It's an often overlooked area, but displayability, as we've said, is becoming a seriously meaningful component to the collector's formula for appreciation. Given the dynamics of this important fictional hero, it's not that impossible to create a mind-boggling and beautiful showcase of Shadow memorabilia.

Start small. Take a 1930s pulp such as the classic "Charg. Monster" issue with The Shadow's hand holding a .45 automatic, his finger encrusted with his fabled "Fire Opal" ring. If you place this pulp in front of a small Shadow sign or a modern-day Graphitti Designs cold porcelain statuette with crossed guns, decorated with a matching Hubley .45 cap pistol and a G.A.R.C.'s red stone Shadow ring and look what you've got.

Look for bargains in unusual collector's items such as old-time radio magazines, movie serial pro-

Creating a knock-out Shadow display. Statuette is less than $200, ring under $200, pulp (a little ragged but nice) under $200 and the Hubley gun under $300—total display is less than $900.

mo pieces (especially 1940 originals), Monogram color cards and posters from 1946, art deco offers, envelopes, salesman brochures, maps from the Perfect-O-Lite campaign (the sponsor only aired five shows ca. 1932), later Shadow Comics with classic covers, BLBs, strips (the great Vernon Green leaded his scarce comic strip art with masses of black shadows...one series of panels tells a story with shadows of The Shadow.

Watch out: Shadow rings have been faked. Here's how to tell the real 1941-42 and 1945-46 glow-in-the-dark rings from the fakes: So far, the mailers have not been reproed, so buy the rings mint in mailers; look for a clear strike (on the Blue Coal ring, "The Shadow" name should be deep if the ring is not worn.

Less than $300: What follows are a few goodies in the $300-and-under range. Some of these have sold for four-figure prices, but they are still theoretically findable at bargain prices:

Rex Selections: The Shadow

Item	1999	2004	CF	SF	IF	TF
1. Perfect-O-Lite offer from 1932	$300	$750	10	10	10	30
2. Shadow Comics file copy from 1940s	$300	$650	10	10	10	30
3. Pulp magazine that shows both Shadows' alter egos on cover .	$300	$600	10	10	10	30
4. Pulp magazine with "red Shadow" cover	$300	$750	10	10	10	30
* 5. Green/black/white 1940 serial promo	$100	$350	10	10	10	30
** 6. "The Shadow Returns" 3-sheet . . . . n/a		n/a	10	10	10	30

* Buy it cheap now, frame it and sell it at a show.

** This is a money-in-the-bank piece. It's rare as can be and you can still find it for under a grand.

Shadow Comics #1.

The Shadow Returns" 3-sheet, very rare, but under $1,000!

On everybody's wish list are these Shadow premiums in the mailers in mint condition. These are from the collection of Les Dent who co-wrote a Shadow story with Walter B. Gibson.

This 1940 serial promo is a bargain for $100.

History: Sir Arthur Conan Doyle's classic sleuth is inarguably the world's most famous 'tec. His image, that of an intelligent, thin, sharp-nosed face under a deerstalker cap, Meerschaum pipe set firmly in his mouth, is instantly recognizable by almost everyone who has read a book or seen a movie. *A Study in Scarlet* was the first Holmes story Conan Doyle penned; from 1887-1920s, the detective ruled the galaxy of print detectives. Everywhere Holmes appeared—books, on stage, over radio and in silent and sound movies—he was a smash success, with a couple of exceptions: the TV screen and juvenile marketplace (save for the modern-day TV version starring Jeremy Brett that ran on PBS for many years and now runs on the cable station A&E). Holmes was a decidedly adult character and was marketed heavily for the first three decades of the 20th century, but only marginally thereafter. His tele-version was aired as strip-programming in the mid-1950s, and Ronald Howard was miscast. The primary collectible area today is movie posters, because of the amazingly well-done series starring Basil Rathbone and Nigel Bruce. Rathbone literally became Holmes to the movie audiences who saw "Hound of the Baskervilles" and "The Adventures of Sherlock Holmes" in 1939. One-sheets from these pictures sell in the thousands, when they move across the auction block, which is infrequently.

The Buzz: A kind of reverse X-Factor is at work with this character. As noted, in such diverse cases as Buck Roger or Roy Rogers, market heat acts as a catalyst to investibility, But in regard to Holmes, the reserve seems to be true. There is relatively little marketplace buzz on this major star, almost as if collectors have given up hopes of finding anything. More than any of the names listed in these pages, the maxim of "buy only what you personally love" would seem to apply, I've listed a few Holmes items where I think some margin exists for a mainstream Sherlock fan.

Buy it now: Any b&w ads, promos, heralds, handbills, anything from "Baskervilles" or "Adventures" if it is original and less than $200. This is a tough character to pursue, but diligence pays off: A TV show of recent years included a segment featuring a private collection of Sherlock material that

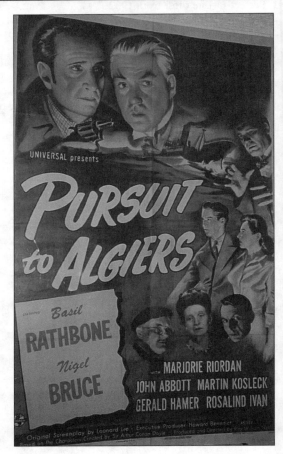

"Pursuit to Algiers" 1-sheet, $750.

From left: Sherlock Holmes premium postcards ($300), Sherlock Holmes and the Rum-Soaked Crooks cigar box label ($400) and Sherlock Holmes Souvenir box ($350).

staggered the senses. The man must have amassed 200 or more figural pieces along, including small statuettes, salt & peppers, and many appeared to be old. Where did he find them? England, presumably, Dr. Watson.

Buy it later: Repros of 1-sheets, tea pots, dinner services, matchbooks, garden tools, etc.

Rex Selections: Sherlock Holmes

Item	1999	2004	CF	SF	IF	TF
* 1. Sherlock Holmes Map of London	$500+	$1,000+	10	11	10	31
2. Sherlock Holmes Detective Disguise Outfit, 1935	$400	$800	10	11	10	31
3. "Pursuit to Algiers" 1-sheet, good visuals, not too pricey	$750	$1,000	10	10	10	30
4. Sherlock Holmes Secret Code Writing Set, 1946	$400	$650	10	10	10	30
** 5. Sherlock Holmes and the Rum-Soaked Crooks cigar box label	$400	$750	10	10	10	30
6. "Sherlock Holmes in the Scarlet Claw" color card, a bargain	$400	$700	10	10	10	30
*** 7. Sherlock Holmes premium postcards, each	$300	$550	10	10	10	30
8. Sherlock Holmes Souvenir box, 1930, Gillette in-person tribute item, unused, fully marked and dated interior	$350	$500	10	10	9	29
9. Sherlock Holmes George Washington Coffee Books 1 and 2, VHTF radio premiums, each	$350	$500	10	10	9	29
**** 10. Sherlock Holmes product label, color galley proof	$275	$400	10	10	9	29

* There are two of these but the one issued HFC as a 1930s radio premium is very rare. I've only seen photos of this piece and I've been buying radio locale maps for 30 years. My best estimate as to current value is $500 or more.

** This sounds like a film title, but it is a cigar box label with stage actor William Gillette's familiar pose in a decorative gilt wreath.

*** Several color giveaway items exist from the turn of the century through the 1940s for products from shoe soles to tires; the average price is $300.

**** This is a file copy of a piece used for clothing, tobacco and other products bearing the Holmes' image, and with the standard Gillette photo.

This Sherlock Holmes Detective Disguise Outfit from 1935 is valued at $400.

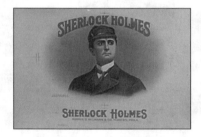

Sherlock Holmes product label, color galley proof, $275.

Sherlock Holmes Secret Code Writing Set, 1946, $400.

History: One of the last and best of the Burtt-Moore-type aviation heroes was former-Navy air-ace Sky King, who kept a bird's eye view of The Flying Crown Ranch, from his Beechcraft Bonanza, The Songbird. Sky's nemesis, when the show first aired in 1946, was a shadowy bad guy named Dr. Shade. One of the primary announcers was Mike Wallace who pitched us what seemed like an endless series of rings: glow-in-the-dark, message, Indian and picture versions, even some that kids called "knucklebusters." Most of these rings sell in the $400 range today in original condition. The Sky King premiums from radio were tightly woven into the show's ongoing plots, much in the manner of the early Jack Armstrong offers, and sad indeed was the kid who failed to obtain the needed proofs-of-pur-chase from Peter Pan Peanut Butter. Derby Foods, Admiral and Nabisco continued to sponsor the show in the transitional radio/TV years of the early- to mid-1950s.

The Buzz: This character's memorabilia has lost much of its investibility. Top "detecto" premiums such as the Microscope Kit complete with accessories, the Secret Signalscope and the gold and silver Spy Detecto Writers will bring $400 and up, but pieces like the Cowboy Tie on card have dropped back to the $100 range. Sky is no longer sky high, prototypes excepted. Oddly enough, there was never a Sky King serial, BLB or—with the exception of a one-shot piece—a radio-era comic book about the flying cowboy.

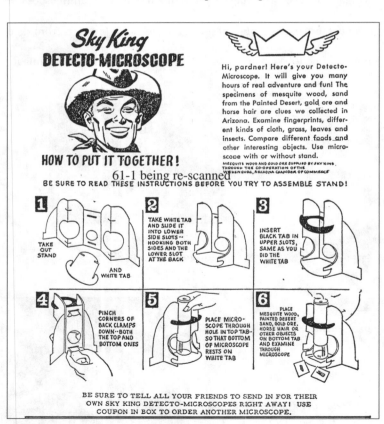

Sky King Microscope Kit.

History: Nearly every famous personality, cartoon or comic character, radio show or film classic generated sheet music of some kind. In the Golden Age, the hallmark of a middle-class American home was an upright piano (often in need of tuning) and a collection of sheet music. As the supply of scarcer collectibles continues to diminish, these once-common artifacts will come back to life.

Buy it now: If you have some favorite characters, seek out anything related to those names. Colorful sheets are still findable from $10-$20, and that includes some of the rarest pieces! The lack of marketplace buzz on the entire category assures us of a good margin for the future, at least where character completists are concerned. Song sheets may never reach stratospheric price heights, but they are nicely affordable pieces for mainstream collectors. Give special attention to major film titles such as "Casablanca," "Gone With the Wind," "Snow White," "Wizard of Oz" and so on.

'20s & '30s Strip Stars: These sheets are all in about the same ballpark. They are still findable for $50 or less, but have brought prices in the low hundreds, where auction competition of prime-condition merchandise strengthened the pieces dramatically. Such pieces have potential $200-$300 capabilities, but still sell for $100 or less. They include: Alley Oop, Barney Google, Bringing Up Father (Jiggs and Maggie), Dick Tracy, Felix the Cat, The Gumps, Harold Teen, Katzenjammer Kids/Captain and the Kids, Krazy Kat, Little Nemo, Little Orphan Annie, Moon Mullins, Mutt & Jeff, Popeye, Skeezik, Smitty, Yellow Kid and so on. Every strip imaginable, from the obscure to mainstream, will also cross-over into the following category:

'20s, '30s & '40s Radio, Feature Film and Animation Stars: There are two distinct sub-groups in this category—the very hot pieces (cartoon animals and horror stars) and titles with little mainstream interest. In the first sub-group, we find Mickey Mouse, Charlie McCarthy, Woody Woodpecker, Snow White, Gene Autry's Melody Ranch and Radio Ranch music, and such oddball items as "You'll Find Out" (a Kay Kyser radio movie with Boris Karloff, Bela Lugosi and Peter Lorre on the cover of a song sheet). The second sub-group finds various

"Wizard of Oz," $200 and up.

Note the famous horror actors on "You've Got Me This Way," $100 and up.

Amos 'n' Andy themes, Big Broadcast titles, Bing Crosby, Bob Hope, George Burns and Gracie Allen, Eddie Cantor, Jack Benny, The Lone Ranger and so on. Both sub-groups sell at varying prices, but pieces in the second sub-group rarely sell for more than $150 a unit, even at big auctions; more typically, they sell in the lower double-digits. Investibility on such items is modest.

Rex Selections: Sheet Music

Item	1999	2004	CF	SF	IF	TF
1. Adventures of Superman	$275	$550	10	10	10	30
* 2. Wizard of Oz, 1939 only	$200	$500	10	10	10	30
3. Casablanca (WWII), "Play it, Sam," Bogart to Dooley Wilson	$200	$450	10	10	10	30

* Never buy re-release material. Also, compare an "Over the Rainbow" sheet picturing the cast, cost-wise, with a rather beat up condition Deluxe Campaign Book from the same film, which last sold for over $2,000. The prices speak for themselves.

Gene Autry sheet music, $100 and up.

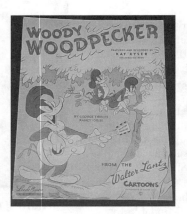

Woody Woodpecker sheet music, ranges from $20 to $120!

"The Big Broadcast of 1937" sheet music.

Bing Crosby and Popeye on the same sheet music!

This Harold Teen sheet music ranges widely in value.

Various stars are featured on this sheet, including Milton Berle. It's a $10 item.

63 Snow White & The Seven Dwarfs

History: All of us whose delightful labors of love take place in the dreamfields of character collectibles rhapsodize over Disney—and for just cause. His genius concepts have never been equaled, and Snow White is as good as it gets. Memorabilia from this landmark title, the first animated feature movie, exists in great number and *most* smalls are not good investments, although a few pins and related items are $500-$1,000 exceptions. Large store displays, original art and peripheral material, complete boxed figure and doll sets with accessories, cereal and other product premiums with containers are all hot. Original cels have gone beyond the reach of most collectors now.

The Buzz: Examples of mid-range pieces with super-strong Investibility include the Pepsodent Movie Picture Machine with cartoon pictures (unassembled in original package), the Snow White Cereal Bowl offer with store display, unusual signage, choice radio sets and any original color items from the 1937 release.

Buy it now (if you can afford it): Cels have been bringing anywhere from $3,000 to $30,000 in recent sales. By the time you read this, the high end will doubtless have moved even higher.

Watch out: This great feature was "The Gone With the Wind" of animation, and it's been re-released with tons of new paper. Do your homework on the color process, as only the real Snow White looks like the original, and in the world of re-releases, repros and fakes, this is a sure way to protect yourself.

This Snow White color test, cel size, 1937, is valued at $2,350.

Snow White target game is a good buy at $450.

Rex Selections: Snow White & The Seven Dwarfs

Item	1999	2004	CF	SF	IF	TF
1. Color poster, 41 inches, 1937	$3,500	$6,000	10	10	10	30
2. Color test, cel size, 1937	$2,350	$3,500	10	10	10	30
3. Shield poster, 24 inches, 1938	$1,750	$3,000	10	10	10	30
4. Pepsodent Cartoon Machine in mailer, complete with 1930s print offer and unpunched parts	$800	$1,500	10	10	10	30
5. Shooting game with pop-up targets, Chad Valley, 1937-38	$450	$750	9	10	9	28

CF-Collectibility Factor; SF-Scarcity Factor; IF-Investibility Factor; TF-Total Factor

Space Patrol & Space Cadet

History: Along with Captain Video and a handful of lesser lights, two vintage shows shared TV network air in the early-1950s. While unrelated, they are linked in collecting. "Tom Corbett—Space Cadet" is often regarded as "Space Patrol's" stepbrother. Some of the collectibles reinforce this: One version of Marx's Sparkling G-Man Gun is rubberstamped "Space Cadet" on the lid, as if the character tie-in was a hasty afterthought.

The Buzz: Store displays, ray guns and rocket ships remain hot and highly investible. Most plastic and paper premiums and store items, including cereal boxes and rings, have yet to reach their marketplace expectations.

Buy it later: Rings, periscopes, binoculars and coloring books, unless you are comfortable with the price. These kinds of things exist in quantity and hoards still turn up.

Watch out: At one time, a couple of actual Space Patrol Terra V rockets existed. They may or may not have rusted away in America's junkyards, but one of these full-size pieces, restored, could bring an unearthly price today. "Spaceman's Luck!"

Tom Corbett, Space Cadet Usalite-Rockhill Countertop Display with Rocket-Lite Rocket Ships and Squadron Cards on header, has a value of $1,500-$3,000.

Exterior of the Space Patrol Auto-Sonic Rifle, which is worth $1,500 complete in mint box.

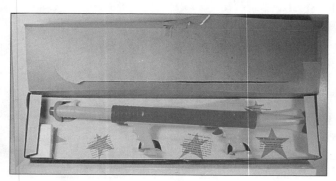

Auto-Sonic Rifle.

Rex Selections: Space Patrol & Space Cadet

Item	1999	2004	CF	SF	IF	TF
* 1. First-tier items	$1,500+	$3,000+	10	10	10	30
** 2. Second-tier items	$1,000	$2,000	10	10	10	30

* These top-of-the-line items share the same values—$1,500-$3,000—but the top bracket will move up sharply. How far is anyone's guess. When I wrote this, John Glenn was preparing to fire his retros, which may or may not signal an unparalleled resurgence of collector demand for such items as: Space Patrol Lunar Fleet Base with mailer, unused; Space Patrol Auto-Sonic Rifle in box; Tom Corbett, Space Cadet Silver Atomic Rifle in box; Space Patrol hanging sign store display with Terra V; Tom Corbett, Space Cadet Usalite-Rock-hill Countertop Display with Rocket-Lite Rocket Ships and Squadron Cards on header; costumes and so on.

** Second-tier items such as Terra V Rockets, filmstrip and mailer; Tom Corbett (printed label version) Sparkling Gun; red and green Cosmic Smoke Guns from Space Patrol (oddly, one of the few major premium toys to have nose-dived in value, the X-Factor working in reverse!).

This Tom Corbett Sparkling Gun is a stiff in today's market.

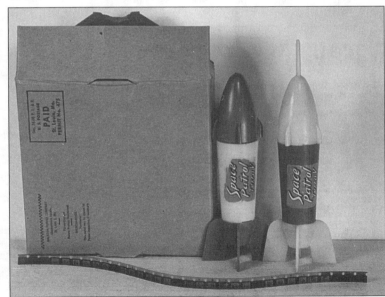

Space Patrol Terra V Rockets, $1,000.

History: The first character called "The Spider," aside from silent movie-era villains, was a top-hatted sleuth, not unlike Arsene Lupin, and national audiences saw his early talkie the same year the first Shadow pulp appeared, in 1931. The Shadow of the short-lived Robert Hardy Andrews series was similarly depicted in print material. The feature movie was based on an obscure stage show (directed by William Cameron Menzies, with the lead played by perennial screen detective Edmond Lowe). "The Spider Strikes," created by R.T. Scott, began in his own pulp mag in 1933. He was by far the craziest of all the pulp protagonists, and his exploits were characterized by some of the worst over-the-top writing ever, but his shtick (a secret identity, a penchant for weird disguises and a ring to leave a spider imprint on the bad guys) was strong.

The Buzz: The Spider's sendaway premiums from the pulp were pricey, even in the shadows of World War II—25 cents in coin or stamps. But such offers, mint in the mailers, are worth $5,000-$10,000 today.

Buy it later: Paper from the second Spider "Returns" serial is pretty but pretty worthless. Thou-

Here is an ad for The Spider Mechanical Pencil with Rubber Stamp Seal in mailer, which sells for $5,000+.

sands of handbills exist, found by an Ohio entrepreneur. "The Spider's Web" paper is in great demand.

Watch out: Spider rings have been reproed and faked.

1931 feature-film wimdow card.

Ad for The Spider League for Crime Prevention Ring. The ring, in original mailer, sells for $5,000+ today.

Rex Selections: The Spider

Item	1999	2004	CF	SF	IF	TF
* 1. The Spider League for Crime Prevention Ring in mailer	$5,000+	$10,000+	10	11	10	31
2. The Spider Mechanical Pencil with Rubber Stamp Seal in mailer	$5,000+	$10,000+	10	11	10	31
3. "The Spider's Web" 3-sheet poster, 1938	$7,500+	$10,000+	10	10	10	30
4. *The Spider Magazine*, #1 issue, 1933	$750+	$1,200+	10	10	10	30
** 5. "The Spider," feature-film window card, 1931	$700+	??	10	11	5	26

* Insist on a two-step provenance with this ring.

** One of the only character collectibles I can think of with a Scarcity Factor so high it's off the charts, but with relatively nil Investibility Factor. It's still among the most beautiful pieces of poster art imaginable.

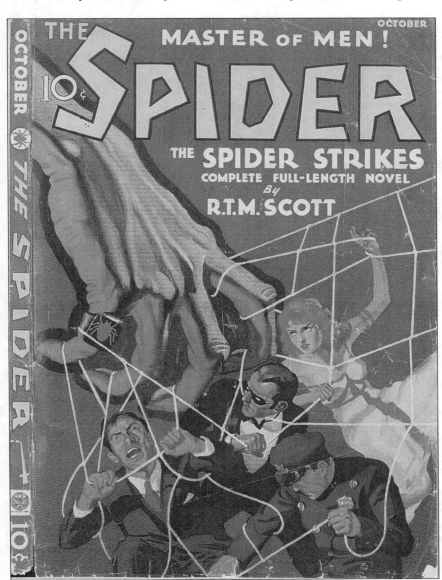

The first Spider pulp magazine from 1933 is valued at $750 or more.

History: Created in-house by Fawcett Publications in 1940, Spy Smasher is a curiosity—another major superstar of the comics and chapter plays who remains way undervalued in the mainstream. Hard-core hero hobbyists are hip, however, that Spy Smasher is smokin' hot!

The Buzz: An amazing collectible came up for grabs at a recent comic character auction. Sotheby's sold a piece of original art for the cover of "Spy Smasher Comics #4" from the estate of Irving Steinbert. It's the only Spy Smasher cover that I've seen go across the auction block in 30 years. I bid 3-large and didn't get near it. This piece is worth 10-grand if it's worth a dime, insofar as a future projected value.

Original art for the cover of "Spy Smasher Comics #4" sold for $5,000. (photo courtesy of Sotheby's)

Spy Smasher color portrait ("Death to Spies!"), is a $500 item in mint condition.

Rex Selections: Spy Smasher

Item	1999	2004	CF	SF	IF	TF
* 1. Spy Smasher 1-sheet mounted on linen	$1,750	$3,000+	10	10	10	30
2. Spy Smasher color portrait ("Death to Spies!"), HTF in mint	$500	$1,000	10	10	10	30
3. Spy Smasher Victory Battalion Membership Kit	$200	$400	10	10	10	30
** 4. "I am a Spy Smasher" pinback	$175	$300	10	10	10	30

Item	1999	2004	CF	SF	IF	TF
5. Spy Smasher "Dell Fast Action" book	$150	$300	10	10	10	30
6. Victory Battalion Membership Card	$100	$200	10	10	10	30
7. Spy Smasher pinback, mint	$70	$120	10	9	10	29
8. Spy Smasher welcomed to the screen by Captain Marvel, framed	$75	$150	10	9	10	29
9. Spy Smasher war-time mini comic	$55	$75	10	8	8	26
*** 10. Spy Smasher issue of *Monsters and Heroes Magazine* . . .	$45	$75	10	10	8	28

* This item was signed by William Witney, who was <u>the</u> director of Republic's comic character serials. A major item. Collector Joel Jacobs is the lucky owner of this phenomenal piece.

** This pinback was accompanied by a letter from Don Winslow of the Navy. It is an unusual cross-over tie-in. Larry Zdeb is another lucky collector.

*** This issue featured several heroes, among them was Spy Smasher. It's a HTF classic fanzine from the mid-1960s.

Warning! Someone out there is making this Spy Smasher belt buckle as we speak.

Spy Smasher 1-sheet mounted on linen is valued at $1,750 today, $3,000 in 2004.

For $75, you can buy this Spy Smasher being welcomed to the screen by Captain Marvel

History: The agency-produced character virtually died with the end of old-time radio, around 1952, a casualty of the Korean War and the advent of TV. Nabisco and the comic book company still got some mileage out of Straight Arrow into the mid-1950s, but his time had come and gone. Around 1949, when the show was a year old or so, we sent away box-tops of Official Tribal War Drums, so we could sing along with the N-A-B-I-S-C-O drumbeat theme. This was at some serious personal cost, because to get the box top a kid actually had to ingest Shredded Wheat, which had the consistency of mattress stuffing.

The Buzz: Straight Arrow is hard to sell, to all but a few kids who remember sending away for Golden Nugget or Magic Cave rings, which you can still get for $15 or so. Unless you run across a Nabisco store sign, display with the cereal box, a pile of Straight Arrow comics with the neat ads in them or a piece of Frank Frazetta original art, you won't find too much investibility here. A few pieces such as coloring book and a couple of target games seem to be about the only store items for Straight Arrow. These items sell from $100-$400, if you find a buyer. Straight Arrow "Injun-uities" belonged to a time when nobody heard of the phrase "politically incorrect."

This Straight Arrow (Nabisco Shredded Wheat) cereal box is valued at $300.

History: Writer Jerry Siegel envisioned Superman's antecedent in the early-1930s, and prefigured him in print in the 1933 mimeographed fanzine *Science Fiction* (five issues were recently auctioned by Sotheby's for $17,000). Siegel and Shuster's Supe appeared in the first issue of Action Comics in 1938. In the 1960s, this book in prime grade could have been purchased in the low thousands. Thirty years later, it sells in the low hundreds of thousands.

The Buzz: It's blast-furnace time for this character. He's the brightest star in the character collectibles firmament.

Rings: Unless you can steal the 1940 rings, just stay away from them. These are controversial pieces and a great deal of conflicting information exists about them, not all of which can be correct. They're too expensive to gamble on. I could write a whole section on nothing but four or five rings, but since the least expensive is priced in the many thousands of dollars, I'd say put your money in something more sure—like commodity futures! Just kiddin'. The Superman Silver Crusader is still a findable mint bargain.

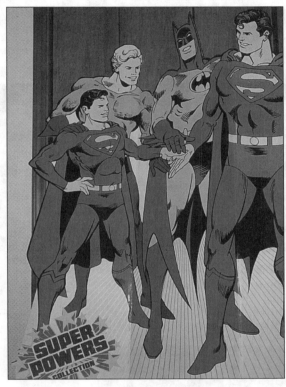

Can't afford the $20,000+ for a superheroes standee from the 1940s? Hope is not lost. Look for this *Superman and Friends* standee from the 1980s that has a $500 solid-gold future.

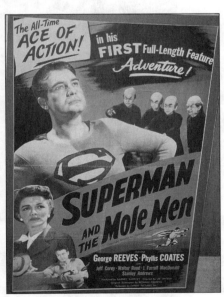

"Superman and the Mole Men" poster, rare, has a $5,750 value.

A pair of Superman red and blue Marx Rollover Planes in boxes will net $12,000.

Rex Selections: Superman

Item	1999	2004	CF	SF	IF	TF
* 1. Superman cartoon standee, Fleischer Studios, 1941-43 . . .	$25,000	$30,000	10	10	10	30
* 2. Superman Chapter Play standee, Columbia, 1948	$20,000	$30,000	10	10	10	30
* 3. Superman "Real Life" comic cover poster, 1948	$15,000	$25,000	10	10	10	30
4. Superman Pep pin, original art and preliminary art, 1944-45	$20,000	$25,000	10	10	10	30
** 5. Superman Pep pin diecut store sign, 1945	$30,000	$35,000	10	10	10	30
6. Pair of red and blue Marx Rollover Planes in boxes	$12,000	$18,000	10	10	10	30
7. Set of large-size comic book portraits, framed	$9,000	$12,000	10	10	10	30
8. War bonds sign using comic book cover art	$10,000	$20,000+	10	10	10	30
9. Supermen of America round patch/mailer/paperwork, HTF	$15,000	$20,000+	10	10	10	30

Box for Superman Play Suit, by Funtime Playwear, with standee, is worth almost $6,000.

Funtime's Superman Play Suit cape.

Funtime's Superman Play Suit standee.

Funtime's Superman Play Suit.

Item	1999	2004	CF	SF	IF	TF
10. Supermen of America rectangular fabric patch/mailer /paperwork	$4,500	$5,000	10	10	10	30
11. Superman cut-out book, unused, 1940	$4,000	$5,000	10	10	10	30
12. Superman costume, 1940	$4,000	$5,000	10	10	10	30
13. Superman Socks box labels, unused, 1949	$3,000	$4,000	10	10	10	30
14. Superman Krypto-Raygun, deluxe version, 1940	$3,000+	$4,000+	10	10	10	30
*** 15. Superman-Tim Club Ring, very fine-plus or better	$4,000+	$7,500+	10	10	10	30
*** 16. Superman-Tim celluloid pin	$2,200	$3,000+	10	10	10	30
17. Superman Krypton Rocket in boxes with accessories	$1,000	$1,500	10	10	10	30
18. Superman Color By Numbers set, sealed in box	$500	$1,000	10	10	10	30
19. Superman Puzzle, several, in box, each	$500	$1,000	10	10	10	30
20. Superman Deluxe Coloring Books, several, each	$300+	$500+	10	10	10	30
21. "Superman and the Mole Men," rarest Superman poster	$5,750	$10,000+	10	10	10	30
22. Superman Golden Muscle Building set, unused and mint	$4,900	$7,200	10	10	10	30
23. Superman Play Suit, by Funtime Playwear, unused with standee	$5,800	$8,000	10	10	10	30
24. Superman Linemar Tank, battery-op, unused in original box	$5,450	$7,500	10	10	10	30

* Superman was the focus of my interest when I began collecting several centuries ago! When I started my mail-order business full time in 1971, I called it "Supermantiques." I've been buying and selling for three decades and I've never found any of these three items.

** There's only one example known to exist. When Sam Gold purchased this piece, there were only 18 pins in the Pep series, which became the most popular Superman item ever made.

*** Superman-Tim was a department store's franchised gimmick to bring kid customers in and keep them happy once they were buying clothes. Secret code stamps and super-manuals were issued monthly between World War II and the Silver Age. A small celluloid pin proclaiming the wearer to be an Official Superman-Tim clubber is typical of an undervalued fragment of future gold. A Superman-Tim ring has an even greater potential to appreciate, particularly in very fine or better investment grade.

Ad for the Superman Krypto-Raygun. Makes you wish you could travel back in time and get this toy for $1!

This deluxe version of the 1940 Superman Krypto-Raygun is worth $3,000 or more.

There are several different Superman Deluxe Coloring Books, each of which is worth $300 or more in top condition.

With original mailer and paperwork, this round and scarce Supermen of America patch is valued at $15,000.

This rectangular Supermen of America fabric patch, with original mailer and paperwork, is a $4,500 item.

In the original box, this Superman Puzzle is valued at $500 or more.

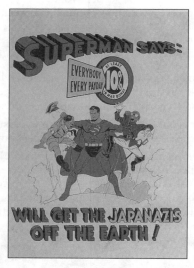

Special posters, like this World War II Bonds Poster, have no theoretical market maximums, as crazy at that might sound. The X-Factor is busy at work again. This poster will likely be valued at more than $20,000 by 2004. (photo courtesy of Sotheby's)

This Superman-Tim celluloid pin is currently a great bargain at $2,200, with the possibility of more than a $3,000 price tag in 2004.

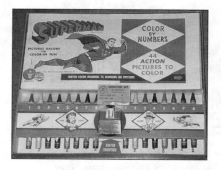

Sealed in box, this Superman Color By Numbers set, is worth $500.

Box for the Superman Krypton Rocket. In complete and mint condition, this sells for about $1,000.

Superman Krypton Rocket.

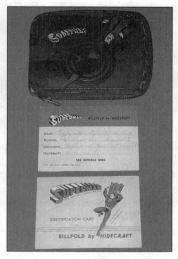

This Hidecraft billfold with ID cards ($400) was a 1947 store item offered by some exhibitors of the 1948 chapter play to lure viewers.

Here is Superman, from a set of large-size comic book portraits which altogether sells for $9,000.

This is an example of a fake Superman belt. The fake is valued at $25.

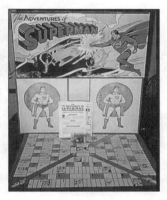

This 1940 Adventures of Superman board game is HFT in pristine mint condition.

You'll have to shell out $375 for this Superman grocery promotional item.

Superman Crayon by Numbers Coloring Set, sealed in box, $500.

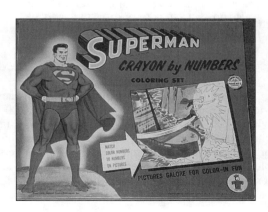

History: "Tarzan of the Apes—A Romance of the Jungle" began in the All-Story pulp in the October 1912 issue and just kept coming. Edgar Rice Burroughs' classic fictional character worked magic in every medium, and the power of the stories has been undiminished by time. The Tarzan legend lives on.

The Buzz: There were many Tarzans and not all were created equal. The Golden Age books and strips contained wondrous, majestic examples of fantasy art taken to its zenith, while, at the same time, there was commercial art that sucked like an Electrolux. You might not know McClurg from Metropolitan from Grossett & Dunlap, or Hogarth from Hacksville, but a quick glance at prime Tarzan artwork in comparison to some dreck like the diecut signs selling Birmingham mid-1930s school supplies, will provide an instant education. If aesthetics have any place in collecting, some of the Tarzan store stuff us hopelessly overpriced. A notorious 1932 radio premium diorama depicts a blond Tarzan with a holstered pistol (the same artist designed a Lone Ranger six-gun with red bullets). Art criticism aside, Tarzan posters, toys and signage will put your kids through college if you buy right. One collector traded some Elmo Lincoln sheets for a new home. But viewed in proportion to the rest of character collecting, there doesn't seem to be much investible margin in these great pieces.

Look for the unusual. Here's a record set of *"Tarzan in the Valley of the Talking Gorillas"* that came in a neat album cover. This one has the mint 78 records inside. Buy it for $100 and sell it for $400. This is the front of the record set.

Back of the record set.

Rex Selections: Tarzan

Posters: Top-line Weissmuller, Lincoln and Merrill posters are valued from $2,000-$20,000, with a 2003 value of $10,000-$50,000. These include classic titles such as "Tarzan of the Apes," one of the best-ever silents, and 1932-34 Weissmullers, plus "Tarzan the Tiger" serial paper. The Total Factor for these items is off the scale! 100? Look for large posters, too. A "Tarzan the Fearless" 1933 24-sheet sold for less than $5,000!

Store displays: These are VHTF and there really isn't a price range. Personally, I'd pay $2,000 for a 1935 Imperial Knife Co., pocket knife display with all 12 knives, mint on store header. I'd double my money when I sold it.

Rare premiums: There are no market ceilings for these items. Fould's Jungleland, complete with stage background and all statuettes and paperwork in the nine different mailing boxes with manual, color chart, etc., etc., is worth at least a couple of grand. Okay, five-grand, but not a penny more!

Archery set: You tell me how much it's worth. I'm clueless. I've never seen one.

Cereal boxes and miscellany: Any vintage item with Tarzan is has a Total Factor of 30. Any of the great-looking box games from the 1930s can still be collected at a reasonable price.

This "Tarzan of the Apes" jig-saw puzzle from 1932 featured a scene from the first Weissmuller Tarzan picture. This envelope with a b&w cut-out photo also offered contest prizes. The puzzle and envelope are valued at $550.

The actual Tarzan jig-saw puzzle.

History: Milton Caniff created the finest of all adventure comic strips in the 1930s. It first saw print starring a kid in knickers named Terry Lee—"a wide awake American boy whose grandfather left him a map of an abandoned mine in China" on Oct. 22, 1934. The original hunt for treasure (see "Board Games" chapter) featured a cast of the two-fisted adventurer Pat Ryan, a pretty girl and her father who ran the treasure boat, along with the ship's cook, Connie. The villain was a half-caste named Poppy Joe. As the hunt evolved into a classic good vs. evil morality play, a character named The Dragon Lady would be introduced. Her personality and the cloud of menace that hovered over Terry would come to dominate the brilliantly crafted storylines. Dari-Rich, Libby's, Penney's and Quaker's offered Golden Age premiums. Terry & the Pirates comics were given away from time to time, but few store items existed (see "Cereal Boxes" chapter).

The Buzz: Other than comics and strips, there is little to collect from the character, even less where The Dragon Lady is concerned (by my count, she appeared on 10 Golden Age items). Excluding the Gold Detector Ring and pencil, I've never seen any radio-era hardware. The various coloring books, small-format books and other cardboard and paper premiums are rather mundane, considering the rich-

Terry & the Pirates set of six glasses in cardboard box carries a value of $200.

ness of the themes and characters. The serial was off the mark, and the TV show was lame in comparison to the radio and comics, but at least they issued a couple of Dragon Lady pieces. Pop-ups and BLBs, Cup Lid and Penny Books, store signs here and there…that's the whole enchilada.

Rex Selections: Terry & the Pirates

Item	1999	2004	CF	SF	IF	TF
1. Store sign, 25 inches, "Copyright 1934 by News Syndicate, Inc."	$3,000	$5,000	10	10	10	30
2. Terryscope Periscope with decoder	$1,000	$1,250	10	10	9	29
3. "Terry's Favorite" store sign with Quaker's box, 1943	$1,000	$1,250	10	10	9	29
4. Terry's comic books display, store sign, three free comics, six bottles in red and yellow Canada Dry Carton, shows Dragon Lady	$1,000	$1,250	10	10	9	29
5. Terry and other characters on Christmas sign, 1930s	$1,000	$1,500	10	10	10	30
6. Terry Victory Plane Spotter in illustrated mailer	$400	$500	10	9	9	28
7. Contest offer on Quaker's sign, 1943	$400	$500	10	10	9	29
8. Set of five Canada Dry pinbacks, with Dragon Lady, 1953	$400	$600	10	9	10	29
9. Quaker Oats set of six pictures with mailer	$400	$500	10	9	9	28
10. Terry & the Pirates set of six glasses in cardboard box	$200	$300	10	9	9	28

The Dragon Lady's Gold Detector Ring.

Terry & the Pirates Q&A

Q: I see a Pirates Gold Detector Ring advertised as being from "Terry & the Pirates," a 1947 radio serial, but in the comic strip ads, there is no proof that it was from that program. What gives?

A: Quaker's sponsored such programs as "Sgt. Preston of the Yukon" (originally "Challenge of the Yukon"), and the Roy Rogers radio show in the 1940s, as well as Terry, and left the ads in the strips generic. But there are several extant transcriptions of the Terry shows in which it is referred to as "The Dragon Lady's Gold Detector Ring."

Q: I have an old radio show where Quaker Oats offers a "Code-Writer," but no one has ever seen this premium. Does it exist?

A: Yes. It was offered about 1943 on radio, but the sponsor was Libby's, so you must have transposed products in your memory. Libby's Tomato Juice, if I recall. It is a four-color lead pencil with a yellow-orange body, and the character of Big Stoop appears on it, along with "Big Stoop's Code-Writer" in Oriental lettering. It was offered during WWII. It's very rare.

Q: I see a Terry & the Pirates Adventure book that is supposedly worth more than $1,000.

A: *The Adventure of Ruby of Genghis* was offered in 1941, also by Libby's. I've heard of it for sale at around $2,000. In its rarest form, it was accompanied by a letter that was actually signed "Terry" in ink, and the letter shows drawings of the radio cast (including the scarcely seen Dragon Lady).

Q: I am hoping to collect premiums and other items from the Terry & the Pirates radio serial. Are there an inexpensive items?

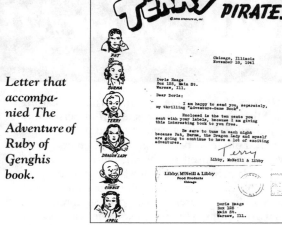

Letter that accompanied The Adventure of Ruby of Genghis book.

A: There were a lot of Golden Age items on which Terry was one of several characters, and these are often bargain priced. While not a radio item, in 1934, the newspaper syndicate put out a color brochure that Terry & the Pirates appeared. Quaker's comic giveaways (contest postcards, etc.), were found by the trillion in a hoard and are usually low priced. Terry was among several shows in which Quaker's offered movie viewers and cartoon film. There was a black set issued in 1939, and one of the few store items I can think of includes Terry cartoons and a two-color viewer with marbleized finished. The best bargain in Terry is probably in reprint comics.

Q: Why didn't Terry & the Pirates have a lot of radio premiums?

A: Quaker's, the primary sponsor in the 1940s, promoted the show heavily, but primarily with contests and prizes rather than the traditional box-top offers. The only clue to what these items are, other than the old scripts or recordings, are the Sunday comic strip advertisements. We see that the show offered airplane pictures, wooden lucky pieces, Armed Services emblems, bikes, radios and tons of prizes—all unmarked. From World War II to the late-1940s, Terry contests were often of the "complete this sentence in 25 words or less" or "complete this Quaker Puffed Wheat jungle" type of contests that were aimed at adults as much as children. In post-war ads, there are occasional examples of sendaways; unless, however, a transcription survives with the premium offered on it, the only proof of a Terry tie-in is the print ad itself. Example: Quaker offered 500 prizes of "Genuine Pictograph Postwar 2-Way Talkie Sets" in 1946. These red and blue items were available to those who sent in the best jingle ideas and "everybody gets a Terry & the Pirates color postcard," the ad assured readers.

History: There were several "Toms," starting with Mix who'd been a top silent film personality and moved (with the advent of sound pictures) into the world of circus performer and entrepreneur. He never played himself on the air, but from the late-1920s and on, he was one of the first stars to do giveaways on a regular basis. A 1930 in-person ad notes that Mix would be giving away "free sombreros and actual gold coins!" In 1933, his name was used by Ralston, American Seed and others when the radio Mix began riding the range in Prescott (later Dobie) County. The radio show generated more than 100 premiums and giveaways. In the mid-1930s, Mascot released a sound serial called "The Miracle Rider," which was also premiumized as one of the Mix Western Movie premiums from Ralston. I spoke with Russ Thorsen who played Mix from 1939-1942, and he recalled being sent a couple of boxes of gun premiums. He told me, "Wooden six-guns and cardboard blowguns with rubber darts. I gave them all away to the kids in my neighborhood and never thought any more about it. Years later, I was told they had become valuable." The post-war Mix was named Curley Bradley, and his voice and style seemed perfected for the part. We listened to the 1940s Mix shows religiously, and badgered Mom to buy Ralston for the coveted boxtops. The memories of running through the night wearing our new model of the glow-in-the-dark arrowhead are unforgettable.

The Buzz: Typical Straight Shooters stuff like secret telephones, telegraph sets and flashlights sell from $150-$350, with a few HTF pieces in the high hundreds, but this is not a character with a strong future, Investibility wise, especially on the more common goods.

Watch out: Be cautious of such pieces as b&w manuals and pamphlets, cigar box labels and any photos signed by Tony the Wonder Horse.

Tom Mix giveaway photo with facsimile autograph.

TV Western Series Collectibles

History: Westerns were some of the first shows on TV. I recall in 1949 or 1950, while a roomful of us kids stared at the Mohawk Rug Test Pattern waiting for Mary Hartline and Super Circus, the shows we most looked forward to were the "Western Adventure Theatre," "Flying W Ranch" and "Action in the Afternoon," the first live Western. TV Westerns were mostly those hardy re-runs of cowpokes like Ken Maynard, John Mack Brown, Bob Steele and company, which were the perfect fit for those 50-minute slots of "Adventure Theatre." The 1950s and 19560s saw some of the best Western programs ever televised. For a while it seemed as if prime-time TV was nothing but variations of "Gunsmoke," with a medical show thrown in here or there. Here are a few of the favorites and an outstanding collectible from that title:

Annie Oakley: Gail Davis had her own lunch box.

Bat Masterson: Gene Barry starred in the pilot episode back in 1958. Soon after, Sealtest made a great cane premium via the mail. The show was a Thursday night fave.

Bonanza: Another big show from the early-1960s that had a lunch box and thermos. Can you see Hoss packing his lunch?

Buffalo Bill Jr. (starred Dick Jones) and **Champion the Wonder Horse** (starred Jim Bannon): These shows were Gene Autry-owned properties from the 1950s. Buffalo Bill Jr., offered a belt and buckle that sell for about $20; Champion's sponsor sent out a toy gun.

Cheyenne: Starred Clint Walker and the pilot aired in September of 1958. There was a board game.

Cisco Kid: These half-hour shows with Duncan Renaldo ran in the early-1950s along with the radio show, and Butter-Nut was among the classic sponsors that issued badges, hats, photos and clicker pistols. Few of these items have significant value aside from a Range War Game premium.

Colt .45: A classic Wayde Preston half-hour from the late-1950s, was one of the program of that period where the character appeared on another show, **Sugarfoot**, for example. Hubley's Colt .45 shadow-boxed gun replica, though not a character

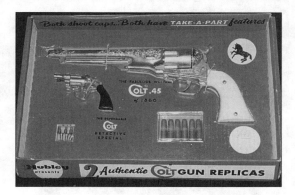

Hubley's Colt .45 shadow-boxed gun replica.

item, per se, is among the most hunted guns. It's a double set with the big revolver in gold, silver and ivory, complete with cartridges, which sells in the thousands of dollars at auction. It is VHTF this set complete in pristine mint.

Davy Crockett: He can be included in the Westerns. Coonskin caps were once as hot as hula hoops.

Death Valley Days: This 1950s show crossed over from old radio and was hosted by personalities such as The Old Ranger and Ronal Regan. The sponsor, Borax, issued a model kit of the 20-Mule Team, which goes for about $50 in the mailer. I can recall my Uncle Art proudly displaying his atop the TV, right above the mirror device over the screen that made the set look large...you had to be there.

The Deputy: This show began around 1959. Can you believe it had henry Fond and Allen Case for the original stars? A badge on the card sells for $40.

The Gabby Hayes Show: It was sponsored by Quaker Puffed Wheat and Rice around 1951. One of the greatest items ever was the enormous knuckle-buster Cannon Ring. Pristine and unused, it's a $400 item today.

Gunsmoke: Starring James Arness, it was one of the longest-running Westerns of all time. Think I'll put on my Seneca Gunsmoke outfit and mosey on over to the Long Branch!

Have Gun, Will Travel: The great Paladin, a portrayed unforgettably by Richard Boone. Peel off

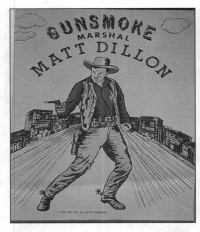

Part of the Matt Dillon costume.

Outside of the box to the Matt Dillon costume, which sells for $145.

Part of the Matt Dillon costume.

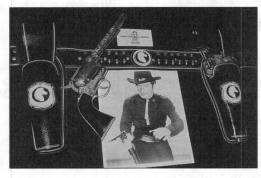

"Have Gun, Will Travel" pair of Hubley Ricochets with chess "knight" logo and complete set of cartridges, will set you back $2,500 or more.

Johnny Ringo gun and holster on the store card.

25 or 30 crisp Ben Franklins to buy the pair of Hubley Ricochets.

Johnny Ringo: (a.k.a., "The Westerners") was a half-hour starring Don Durant as the "fastest, <u>strangest</u> gun in the West!" Pick up his fast-draw rig on the store card while it's "only a few hundred bucks," buckaroo.

The Lawman: Starring John Russell was on by 1959 or so, and was one of the programs tied-in to the Hartland plastic gunfighter series.

The Lone Ranger: This show, with Clay Moore, had been on TV for eight years when General Mills (sponsor since World War II, issued a pair of 6-foot full-color posters of The Lone Ranger and Tonto. A mint pair in the mailer will blast $2,000 into confetti.

"Maverick" and "Roaring 20s" Peter Paul Mounds box.

Maverick and **Roaring 20s:** These shows were sponsored by Peter Paul Mounds in 1962, and there are illustrated boxes helping to promote the shows (as the company did for "Ozzie and Harriet." The

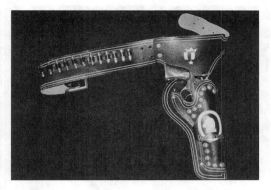

"The Restless Gun" holster set with gun.

"The Restless Gun" cap gun.

boxes aren't real valuable, but they're one of the only items with James Garner's likeness.

The Restless Gun: John Payne was tied to the only art deco cap buster. Complete, mint with holster set, it's a maximum rarity.

"The Rifleman" Hubley's Flip Special in box, valued at $2,500 or more.

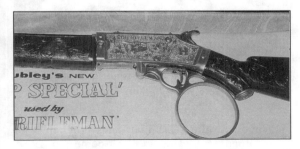

Close-up of "The Rifleman" Hubley's Flip Special.

The Rifleman: From North Fork, as played by Chuck Conners and Johnny Crawford, first bean as

Chuck Conners holds the real deal.

"The Sharpshooter," a 1958 "Zane Gray Theatre" episode. Hubley's Flip Special was a perfect walk-out from the TV show. Boxed and mint, it has had an incredible growth record. In just the last three years, we've seen it climb from $400 to more than $2,500 in an auction war!

Rin Tin Tin ring offer.

Rin Tin Tin: This was a hit TV show in 1954, while it was still on radio. Unique Among character collectibles, not even Lassie can claim to have been played by more than 100 actors, albeit, four-legged. Tinny ruled silent films, chapter—he was the "mascot" in Mascot Serials—barked his way to one of the first adventure radio series, etc. A set of 1955 Nabisco plastic rings, store, ad, Rice Honey's cereal flat, premium gun, belt and holster brought $1,000. Woof!

Shotgun Slade: Starring Scott Brady, this 30-minute show is from 1959 and produced such smalls as puzzles that sell from $15-$25, coloring books and the like. I'd guess there's a toy shotgun around, but I haven't run across it.

Sugarfoot: An hour Will Hutchins show aired initially in 1957, and a gun set was produced, but collectors are particularly interested in the videocassettes of the show itself, as it was legendary for spin-offs, crossovers, famous actor cameos and so on. One sees the various stars and characters from other Westerns such as "Bronco," "Colt .45" and "Maverick" interacting with the "Sugarfoot" cast. "Maverick" collectibles include classic spoofs of other shows such as "Bonanza" and "Gunsmoke," and they still hold up as good entertainment today.

Tales of Wells Fargo: Initially aired with the gravel-voiced Dale Robertson starring in "A Tale of Wells Fargo," a 1956 episode of "Schlitz Playhouse." Variations of the show ran into the 1960s, and you can find boxed board games, gun-and-holster sets, cowboy and cowgirl apparel, lunch boxes and thermoses, statuettes and a couple of dozen episodes surviving on video. One item, a Pall Mall Cigarette sign, sold for nearly $300.

The outside of the Halco gun and holster set box, valued at $500 or more.

The Texan: This show is representative of the wealth of Western and adventure character shows on TV from the early-1950s to the 1970s, that lent the show's title or the primary character's name to the collectible merchandise. This entire field is exploding now and is one of the great growth areas in character collectibles where you can still find bargains. Mint or near mint store stock, boxed, however, will

Halco gun and holster set.

almost always generate a small bidding battle when sold at auction. "The Texan" is a rather obscure program that starred Rory Calhoun, who appears in the colorful window box of the gun set shown, and these Halco sets are not top of the line. The guns might be Pintos, Rodeos or other generic types, and the leather or leatherette holster sets were no very outstanding, but the last three store stock sets sold brought $450, $540 and $555 in original condition..

Wagon Train six-shooter has shot up in valued over the past few years to more than $1,000.

Wagon Train: This hour-long program with Ward Bond first came in U.S. homes in 1957. Bond's show-biz pal Duke Wayne and other famous actors appeared in supporting roles. Radio stalwart John McIntire took over the lead role in the 1960s when 90-minute formats were airing. There were several great artifacts made, notably a revolving-cylinder six-gun set with cartridges and a gorgeous metallic patina. Like "The Rifleman's" flip special, a shadow-boxed mint six-gun has shot up from the mid-hundreds to the thousand-dollar range.

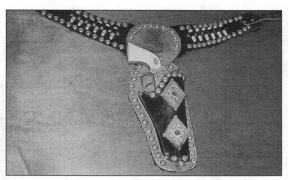

"Wild Bill Hickok" six-gun and holster set with cartridges, $500.

One version of "Wanted: Dead or Alive" gun.

"Wild Bill Hickok" Jigsaw, $50.

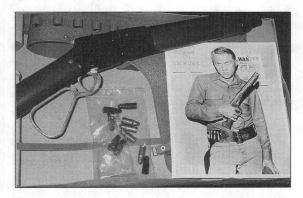

Another version of "Wanted: Dead or Alive" gun. This one sold for more than $2,000.

Wanted: Dead or Alive: With all-time great Steve McQueen, the show first aired at "The Bounty Hunter" on an episode of "Trackdown" in 1958. A complete set of Marx "Mare's Laig" guns, boxed and carded, went to $2,061 when the hammer fell.

Wild Bill Hickok: This was an early-1950s success for Kellogg's, with Guy Madison and Andy Devine as "Jingles." *Hey, Wild Bill, wait for me!* There's a ton of stuff and prices run the gamut: jigsaw ($50), ranch bunkhouse ($25), Jingles cereal box with guns on back ($275); Deputy Marshall photo badge, ID and case ($125); postcard photo

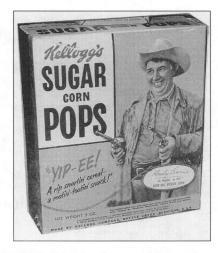

"Wild Bill Hickok" Jingles cereal box with guns on back, $275.

($15); 1953 treasure map, secret guide and uncut box with offer ($350); ornate riveted leather six-gun and holster set with cartridges ($500).

Wyatt Earp: Premiering in 1955, this 30-minute Western starred High O'Brian. Hubley and others made long-barreled Buntline Specials, which sell for $250 uncarded and $450 carded.

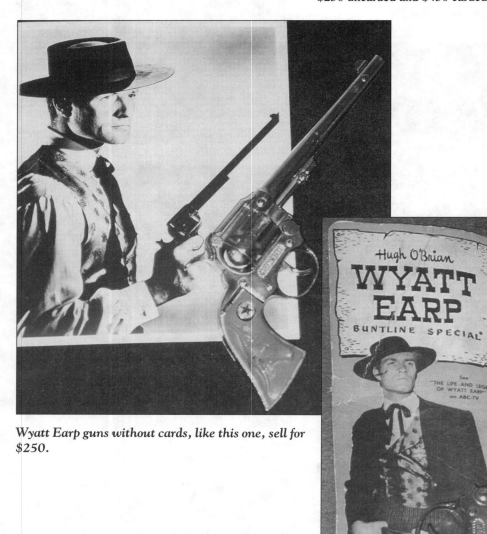

Wyatt Earp guns without cards, like this one, sell for $250.

Wyatt Earp Hubley gun.

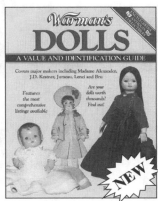

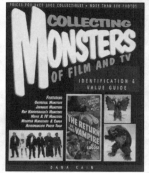

ToyShop *Is Open!*

Come on in! *Toy Shop* opens endless possibilities for great buys and fair deals for buyers and sellers, collectors and dealers. Browse with thousands from coast to coast! Plus, you get great news articles that will fill you in on the latest in the world of toys.

★ THE HOBBY'S #1 MARKETPLACE ★

★ THOUSANDS OF ADS - CLASSIFIED AND DISPLAY ★

★ AUCTIONS ★ SHOWS ★ TRAVELERS DIRECTORY ★

26 BIG ISSUES A YEAR FOR JUST $33.98!

SUBSCRIBE NOW!

SAVE $69.50 OFF THE SINGLE COPY PRICE!

Krause Publications
700 E State St, Iola, WI 54990-0001